Athletics Investigation Handbook
(2015 Edition)

Athletics Investigation Handbook
(2015 Edition)

A GUIDE FOR INSTITUTIONS AND INVOLVED PARTIES DURING THE NCAA ENFORCEMENT PROCESS

Michael L. Buckner

ATHLETICS INVESTIGATION HANDBOOK (2015 EDITION)
A GUIDE FOR INSTITUTIONS AND INVOLVED PARTIES
DURING THE NCAA ENFORCEMENT PROCESS

iUniverse books may be ordered through booksellers or by contacting:

iUniverse
1663 Liberty Drive
Bloomington, IN 47403
www.iuniverse.com
1-800-Authors (1-800-288-4677)

ISBN: 978-1-4917-6119-9 (sc)
ISBN: 978-1-4917-6121-2 (hc)
ISBN: 978-1-4917-6120-5 (e)

Library of Congress Control Number: 2015902888

Print information available on the last page.

iUniverse rev. date: 03/10/2015

CONTENTS

PART 3

PART 4

APPENDIX A

APPENDIX B

To athletic administrators, coaches, and collegiate athletes who strive to uphold the treasured principles of higher education and intercollegiate athletic competition.

PREFACE

In my career as a sports attorney, I have represented colleges, universities, coaches, and student-athletes in legal and administrative matters involving the National Collegiate Athletic Association. The cases ranged from student-athlete eligibility issues to high-profile NCAA enforcement investigations pertaining to unethical conduct, improper benefits, academic fraud, and violations of policy on performance-enhancing drugs. My clients' reputations can be damaged if a case goes south, or they can be vindicated with a win. My clients rely on my experience as an attorney, a former licensed private investigator, and a former NCAA consultant to guide them through the NCAA's complex investigative processes. I decided to write a book summarizing my knowledge of the NCAA enforcement process to help others who have been accused of violating NCAA rules. *The Athletics Investigation Handbook (2015 Edition): A Guide for Institutions and Involved Parties during the NCAA Enforcement Process* is the result of my efforts.

This book, the second edition, is primarily designed for college administrators, coaches, athletic conference commissioners, attorneys, private investigators, and other professionals involved or associated with the NCAA enforcement process. *The Athletics Investigation Handbook* provides internal investigation strategies and techniques, best practices, formats for institutional reports, and suggested citation forms for NCAA member institutions and involved individuals appearing before the NCAA infractions committees and infractions appeals committees. This project was initiated to provide institutions and involved individuals a comprehensive guide for conducting internal investigations. *The Athletics Investigation Handbook* is also intended to increase the integrity of the enforcement process before the infractions committees by encouraging the submission of better manuscripts that will advance scholarship and improve policy in the NCAA and in higher education. Member institutions and involved individuals should use this book in conjunction with information received from their athletic conferences, the NCAA enforcement staff, the committees on infractions, and the infractions appeals committees.

ACKNOWLEDGMENTS

This project would not have been possible without the support and encouragement of my wife, family, friends, and colleagues. I owe a debt of gratitude to all those who served as sounding boards and sources of wisdom and whose observations improved this work greatly.

The 2015 Edition of this book was prepared through the careful research assistance of interns Andrea Siluk (summers of 2013 and 2014) and Erica Glick (summer of 2013).

INTRODUCTION

The 2015 Edition of *The Athletics Investigation Handbook* provides updated information reflecting the numerous procedural and structural changes in the NCAA enforcement process. The book contains the following features to help NCAA member institutions and involved individuals conduct internal investigations, respond to NCAA allegations, and prepare for infractions hearings during the NCAA enforcement process:

- The NCAA and the Enforcement Process (part 1) provides an overview of the NCAA and its members and staff as well as a summary of the NCAA enforcement process.
- Internal Investigations (part 2) provides an explanation of internal investigation strategies and techniques for institutions and involved individuals.
- Best Practices, Report Formats and Citations, and Investigation Resources (part 3) provides a list of best practices concerning internal investigations, format and citation suggestions for institutional reports, and a list of investigative books, firms, contacts, and resources.
- Guide to Committee on Infractions Procedural Decisions (part 4) provides a summary of evidentiary and procedural decisions (through December 31, 2014) of the committees on infractions and infractions appeals committees.
- The appendices feature a glossary, checklists, and a directory of investigative resources.

PART 1

THE NCAA AND THE ENFORCEMENT PROCESS

CHAPTER 1

NCAA MEMBERSHIP, THE ENFORCEMENT STAFF, AND THE COMMITTEES ON INFRACTIONS

During the NCAA enforcement process, member institutions and involved individuals interact on one or more occasions with the NCAA enforcement staff, the committees on infractions, the infractions appeals committees, and athletic conference officials. This section provides a brief description of these groups and their role in the NCAA enforcement process.

The NCAA and NCAA Member Institutions

The National Collegiate Athletic Association ("NCAA" or the "Association") is a voluntary organization of about 1,200 colleges and universities, athletic conferences, and affiliated sports organizations devoted to the "sound administration of intercollegiate athletics" (NCAA n.d.). A *member institution* is a college or university with one of three categories of membership (active, conference, and affiliated) in the association (NCAA Constitution 3.01, 3.02.3.1, 3.02.3.2, and 3.02.3.3). NCAA legislation describes the requirements, rights, and privileges for each membership category (NCAA Constitution 3.02.3). The membership is divided into three *divisions*: Divisions I, II, and III. NCAA Bylaw 20 defines the criteria for membership in each division.

An NCAA member institution employs administrators who have designated responsibilities concerning the operation of its athletic program, including a chief executive officer, director of athletics, faculty athletics representative, senior woman administrator, compliance officer, and other selected administrators.

A *chief executive officer* (e.g., president, chancellor) is responsible for the implementation of the strategic plan and policies established by the institutional or university system board of trustees/regents. The chief executive officer also oversees the institution's operations. Under NCAA legislation, a chief executive officer has the ultimate responsibility and authority for the conduct of an institution's athletic program.

A *director of athletics* is responsible for the operations of an institution's athletic program. A *faculty athletics representative* is a member of an institution's faculty or administrative staff who is designated by the chief executive officer to represent the institution and its faculty in the institution's relationships with the NCAA and its athletic conference (NCAA Constitution 4.02.2). A *senior woman administrator* is the highest-ranking female administrator involved with the conduct of a member institution's athletic program (NCAA Constitution 4.02.4.1). A *compliance officer* coordinates the administration of an institution's athletic compliance program. An institution may employ other administrators with varying titles and responsibilities to assist in the operation of the athletic program.

Athletic Conference

An *athletic conference* is "a group of colleges and/or universities that conducts competition among its members and determines a conference champion in one or more sports (in which the NCAA conducts championships or for which it is responsible for providing playing rules for intercollegiate competition)" (NCAA Constitution 3.02.3.2). A *conference commissioner* oversees the operations of an athletic conference.

NCAA Rules and Athletic Compliance Programs

The NCAA and its membership are governed by the association's constitution, rules, and regulations, called *bylaws* or *legislation*. Bylaws are introduced and voted on by division-specific boards, councils, and committees, which are comprised of representatives from the NCAA membership. Some bylaws are common among all divisions, while others are applicable only to members in a specific division, sub-division or a defined subset within a sub-division (i.e., "Power 5" conferences). (For the purposes of this book, division-specific legislation will be denoted by the applicable division.) The NCAA Constitution and bylaws are published annually in a division-specific *NCAA Manual*. The NCAA Constitution and bylaws can also be accessed on the NCAA website (http://www.ncaa.org).

Member institutions are required to establish a compliance program to ensure that athletic programs adhere to NCAA legislation. In particular, an institution is expected to maintain a centrally coordinated system that ensures effective communication, organization, documentation, and evaluation of its compliance program (Division I Committee on Infractions, 1996, 1–7).

Involved Parties or Individuals

An *involved party* or *involved individual* is a person or organization implicated or named directly or indirectly in an alleged violation of NCAA legislation. Involved individuals can include campus and athletic department administrators (e.g., chief executive officer, director of athletics, vice president), institutional personnel (e.g., faculty, staff), coaches, student-athletes, or representatives of the institution's athletics interests.

A *student-athlete* is a student who: (a) was recruited by an institution or a representative of the institution's athletics interests to participate in the institution's athletic program; or (b) reports for an intercollegiate athletic team that is under the jurisdiction of the institution's athletic program (Bylaw 12.02.10).

A *representative of the institution's athletics interests* ("athletic representative") is an individual, independent agency, corporate entity, or other organization that is known, or that should have been known, by a member of the institution's administration to: (a) have participated in or been a member of an agency or organization promoting the institution's athletic program; (b) have made financial contributions to the athletic department or to an athletic booster organization of the institution; (c) be assisting or to have been requested by athletic staff to assist in the recruitment of prospective student-athlete; (d) be assisting or have assisted in providing benefits to enrolled student-athletes or their families; or (e) have been involved otherwise in promoting the institution's athletic program (Bylaw 13.02.14). Most important, an individual, independent agency, corporate entity, or other organization identified as an athletic representative retains that identity indefinitely (Bylaw 13.02.14.1).

NCAA Enforcement Staff

The stated mission of the NCAA enforcement staff is "to act as a means of accountability for member institutions by seeking out and processing information relating to possible major and secondary violations of NCAA legislation in accordance with the policies and procedures enacted by the NCAA membership" (Enforcement/Infractions, 2004). The *vice president for enforcement services* is responsible for the operations of the NCAA enforcement services group. A team of managing directors and *directors of enforcement* assists the vice president. Directors of major enforcement supervise teams of assistant directors that investigate alleged major violations of NCAA legislation (Enforcement/Infractions, 2004). The enforcement services group have a staff that processes alleged secondary violations of NCAA legislation and a staff that develops information (specifically, with a focus on strategically building knowledge, meaningful contacts and actionable leads to better inform investigations). Further, the enforcement services group assigns individuals to focus on several key areas of emphasis including: agents; football; men's and women's basketball; and sports wagering (NCAA n.d.).

Committees on Infractions and Infractions Appeals Committees

The *committees on infractions* and *infractions appeals committees* are independent bodies composed of individuals from NCAA member institutions, athletic conferences, and the general public. Each NCAA division has its own committee on infractions and appeals committee. The committees are responsible for the administration of the NCAA enforcement program (Bylaw 19.1). A full team of NCAA staff members assist the committees in drafting reports and letters, arranging committee travel, and planning committee meetings (NCAA, n.d.; Enforcement/Infractions, 2004).

The committees have the authority to: (a) consider complaints concerning a member's failure to maintain NCAA academic or athletic standards or membership conditions or obligations; (b) devise and amend policies and procedures for the NCAA enforcement process; (c) establish facts related to alleged violations and discover violations of NCAA legislation; (d) impose an appropriate penalty or show-cause requirement on a member found to be involved in a major violation (or in appeals involving secondary violations), or recommend suspension or termination of membership to the division-specific board of directors or president's council; and (e) carry out any other duties directly related to the administration of the enforcement program (Bylaw 19.3.6).

The Division I Committee on Infractions is composed of not more than 24 representatives from Division I member institutions, athletic conferences and the general public (NCAA Division I Bylaw 19.3.1).

Unless ordered otherwise by the chair of the Committee on Infractions, cases involving Level I or Level II violations will be presented to and decided by hearing panels consisting of not less than five and not more than seven members of the full Committee on Infractions and chaired by a chief hearing officer (NCAA Division I Bylaws 19.3.3 and 19.3.8). For each case set for hearing and in consultation with the chair of the Committee on Infractions, the chief hearing officer designates a panel member or other member of the committee to serve as the committee appeals advocate for any appeal from the decision of the panel (NCAA Division I Bylaw 19.3.8). The committee appeals advocates represent the committee on matters appealed to the Division I Infractions Appeals Committee (NCAA Division I Bylaw 19.3.8). The committee meets up to six times per year for two- or three-day sessions at locations throughout the country (Enforcement/Infractions, 2004).

The Division II Committee on Infractions consists of seven members, including one member of the Division II Management Council and one individual from the general public (NCAA Division II Bylaw 19.1.1). One of the committee members serves as a liaison from the Division II President's Council (Enforcement/Infractions, 2004). The committee meets on an as-needed basis (Enforcement/Infractions, 2004).

The Division III Committee on Infractions is composed of five members, including one member from the Management Council and one member from the general public (NCAA Division III Bylaw 19.1.1). The committee meets on an as-needed basis (Enforcement/Infractions, 2004).

An infractions appeals committee exists in Divisions I, II, and III. The appeals committees are bodies charged with hearing and deciding on appeals concerning the findings of major violations by each division's committee on infractions.

CHAPTER 2

DIVISION I: THE NCAA ENFORCEMENT PROCESS

Introduction

In October 2012, the NCAA Division I Board of Directors adopted an overhaul of the enforcement structure. The revision created additional levels of violations, revamped the investigation process, and enhanced penalties for the most serious rules violations. The new enforcement process for Division I member institutions includes the following features:

- A four-tier violation structure that tops off with "severe breaches of conduct" and sets "incidental infractions" as the lowest violation category. The structure replaces the two-tier approach (major and secondary violations) and is designed to focus most on conduct breaches that seriously undermine or threaten the integrity of the NCAA Constitution and bylaws.
- Head coach responsibility/accountability enhancement as well as potential consequences for head coaches who fail to direct their staffs and student-athletes to uphold NCAA bylaws. The penalties under the new process can include game suspensions ranging from 10 percent of the season to an entire season.
- Division I Committee on Infractions membership increases from ten to as many as twenty-four voting members. Infractions cases are processed by panels of the full committee.
- Penalties (e.g., postseason bans, scholarship reductions, recruiting limits, head coach suspensions, show-cause orders, and financial penalties) that align with the severity of the violations. Further, the new penalty structure emphasizes aggravating and mitigating circumstances in each case.
- Shared-responsibility emphasis, which includes highlighting "a culture among head coaches, the compliance community, institutional leadership and conferences to assume a shared responsibility for upholding the values of intercollegiate athletics."
- The new enforcement process became effective on August 1, 2013. Starting on that date, the NCAA began processing cases by these rules:

- Breaches of conduct (violations) that occurred before October 30, 2012, and were processed before August 1, 2013, were subject to the former process and penalties.

- Breaches of conduct that occurred before October 30, 2012, and were processed after August 1, 2013, were subject to the new process; however, such cases would incur the more lenient of the two penalty structures.

- Breaches of conduct that occurred before and after October 30, 2012, and were processed after August 1, 2013, would be subject to the new process and the revised penalties as long as most of the violations occurred after October 30, 2012.

- Breaches of conduct that occurred after October 30, 2012, and were processed after August 1, 2013, were subject to the new process and the revised penalty structure.

The Four-Tier Violations Structure

Level I: Severe Breach of Conduct

Violations that seriously undermine or threaten the integrity of the NCAA collegiate model as set forth in the constitution and bylaws, including any violation that provides or is intended to provide a substantial or extensive recruiting, competitive, or other advantage, or a substantial or extensive impermissible benefit. Multiple Level II and III violations may collectively be considered a severe breach of conduct.

Level II: Significant Breach of Conduct

Violations that provide or are intended to provide more than a minimal but less than a substantial or extensive recruiting, competitive, or other advantage. Such violations include more than a minimal but less than a substantial or extensive impermissible benefit or involve conduct that may compromise the integrity of the NCAA collegiate model as set forth in the constitution and bylaws. Multiple Level III violations may collectively be considered a significant breach of conduct.

Level III: Breach of Conduct

Violations that are isolated or limited in nature, provide no more than a minimal recruiting, competitive, or other advantage, and do not include more than a minimal impermissible benefit. Multiple or repeated Level IV violations may collectively be considered a breach of conduct.

Level IV: Incidental Infractions

Minor infractions that are inadvertent and isolated, technical in nature, and result in a negligible competitive advantage. Level IV infractions generally will not affect eligibility for intercollegiate athletics.

Revised Procedures to Investigate and Process Alleged Rules Violations

The NCAA enforcement process addresses instances wherein a member institution is in noncompliance with NCAA legislation. Some athletic conferences, including the Pacific-12 Conference, also have formal enforcement processes to review alleged violations of conference and NCAA rules. The enforcement process is designed to be a cooperative program involving member institutions, involved individuals, athletic conferences, and the NCAA enforcement staff to: (a) reduce violations of NCAA legislation; and (b) impose appropriate corrective measures and penalties if violations occurred at an institution.

Initiation of the Enforcement Process

The NCAA enforcement process in Division I is initiated in a number of ways. For example, the NCAA enforcement staff can initiate an investigation when it receives information or an allegation from a media report or an anonymous or nonattributable source (e.g., high-school and college coaches, student-athletes, the general public) concerning a possible violation of NCAA legislation at a member institution. In addition, enforcement staff investigations begin after a member institution discovers and self-reports violations to the staff. Finally, the enforcement staff makes proactive efforts to discover potential violations, including: (a) interviewing highly recruited prospective student-athletes and student-athletes who have transferred from member institutions; or (b) attending selected athletic contests and events (e.g., high-school or two-year college all-star games) that may be attended by college coaches.

When the enforcement staff receives allegations or other information concerning a possible violation of NCAA legislation, the information is evaluated by the staff. If the information pertains to a Level III or IV violation of NCAA legislation, the information may be provided to the member institution or the institution's athletic conference for review and processing under the applicable procedures. If the information is deemed to be of a serious nature (alleged Level I and II violations or multiple Level III violations), it is assigned to an associate or assistant director for a follow-up examination.

The enforcement staff is permitted to start a review of a member institution only when the staff has reasonable cause to believe that the institution may have violated NCAA legislation. If this burden is satisfied, the staff determines whether the possible violation should be reviewed via correspondence with the involved member institution or its athletic conference or whether the enforcement staff should conduct its own in-person inquiries.

Notice of Inquiry and Investigation of Allegations

When the staff receives reasonably reliable information that an intentional violation has occurred, that a significant competitive or recruiting advantage may have been gained, or that false or misleading information may have been reported to the member institution or to the enforcement staff, the staff begins to investigate the information to determine its credibility.

Before the enforcement staff conducts an inquiry on an institution's campus, the staff is required to notify the institution's president or chancellor of the inquiry. The "notice of inquiry" can be made orally or in writing. The notice suspends the statute of limitations for alleged rules violations. The notice explains the institution's "obligation to cooperate and the confidential nature of the inquiry." Further, the notice informs the institution "that if the inquiry develops reliable information of a possible Level I or II violation, a notice of allegations will be produced." The enforcement staff, conversely, could notify the institution "that the matter may be processed as a Level III violation or that the matter has been concluded."

Notice of Allegations and Prehearing Procedures

The enforcement staff conducts investigations for a reasonable period to assess whether information exists that shows evidence of NCAA rules violations leading to a possible Level I or II case. If the staff determines that sufficient information exists to determine that a severe or significant breach of conduct occurred at a member institution, a notice of allegations is sent to the institution's chief executive officer. The document contains a "notice of the alleged violation(s), the details of the allegations, the possible level of each alleged violation, the processing level of the case, the available hearing procedures and the opportunity to answer the allegations. The notice of allegations shall also identify the factual information and aggravating and/or mitigating factors on which the enforcement staff may rely in presenting the case" (Bylaw 19.7.1) The enforcement staff also notifies athletic department personnel and student-athletes—whose employment or athletic eligibility could be affected—of the allegations in a notice of allegations in which they are named.

The institution and involved individuals have ninety days to respond to the notice of allegations. However, the institution and involved individuals may request additional time to respond; the chief hearing officer of a committee on infractions hearing panel grants such extensions. Under Bylaw 19.7.2, the "enforcement staff may establish a deadline for the submission of responses to any reasonable time within the 90-day period, provided the institution and all involved individuals consent to the expedited deadline." If a party fails to "submit a timely response," the panel may view it "as an admission that the alleged violation(s) occurred" (Bylaw 19.7.2). Finally, "an institution or involved individual may not submit additional documentary evidence without prior authorization from the chief hearing officer."

Within sixty days after the institution and involved individuals submit written responses to the notice of allegations, the enforcement staff is required to "submit a written reply to the hearing panel, and pertinent portions to an involved individual or institution" (Bylaw 19.7.3). Further, the enforcement staff must "prepare a statement of the case setting forth a brief history of the case, a summary of the parties' positions on each allegation and a list of any remaining items of disagreement" (Bylaw 19.7.3). Involved individuals will be provided "those portions of the statement in which they are named" (Bylaw 19.7.3).

The enforcement staff will establish a custodial site that contains "recorded interviews, interview summaries and/or interview transcripts, and other factual information" (Bylaw 19.5.9). The site can take the form of a secure website or hard copy of files at the NCAA national office. The enforcement staff will provide the institution and involved individuals with access to the custodial site.

Within sixty days after the institution and involved individuals submit written responses to the notice of allegations, the enforcement staff will conduct prehearing conferences (Bylaw 19.7.4). A prehearing conference involves the enforcement staff consulting with "institutional representatives and other involved individuals in order to clarify the issues to be discussed during the hearing, make suggestions regarding additional investigation or interviews that should be conducted by the institution to supplement its response and identify allegations that the staff intends to amend or withdraw" (Bylaw 19.7.4). The enforcement staff conducts "independent prehearings with the institution and/or any involved individuals, unless mutually agreed by all parties to do otherwise" (Bylaw 19.7.4).

All written material from the institution and involved individuals to be considered by the hearing panel must be received by the hearing panel, enforcement staff, institution, and any involved individuals at least thirty days prior to the date the panel considers the case (Bylaw 19.7.5). This deadline can be revised by an order of the chief hearing officer. However, according to Bylaw 19.7.5, "information may be submitted at the hearing subject to the limitations set forth in Bylaw 19.7.7.3," which states: "At a hearing, the parties of their legal counsel have the obligation to present, to the extent reasonably possible, material, relevant information necessary for the hearing panel to reach an informed decision, including information that corroborates or refutes an allegation. Subject to procedures of the Committee on Infractions, the parties or their legal counsel may deliver opening and closing statements, present factual information, make arguments, explain the alleged violations and answer questions from panel members. Any oral or documentary information may be received, but the panel may exclude information that it determines to be irrelevant, immaterial or unduly repetitious."

Finally, the chief hearing officer has the "authority to resolve procedural matters that arise prior to an infractions hearing" (Bylaw 19.7.6).

Alternate Processing Options for Infractions Cases

An institution and involved individuals can elect to process a Level I or II case using one of four methods:

- Summary disposition (Level I and II cases).
- Expedited hearing (Level II cases).
- Written record (Level II cases).
- Committee on infractions hearing (Level I and II cases).

Summary Disposition (Level I and II Cases)

Eligible member institutions and involved individuals may elect to process a Level I or II case through summary disposition, a procedure used in place of a formal committee hearing. Summary disposition procedures can be used only if "the enforcement staff, involved individuals, if participating, and the institution" agree to the process (Bylaw 19.6.1). Further, under the rules, "the institution, an involved individual or the enforcement staff may require, as a condition of agreement, that the parties jointly submit the proposed findings to the chair of the Committee on Infractions or his or her designee for a preliminary assessment of the appropriateness of the use of the summary disposition process" (Bylaw 19.6.1).

A hearing panel of the committee on infractions shall consider the summary disposition case during a subsequent meeting. Per Bylaw 19.6.4, the hearing panel is permitted to perform one or more of the following actions:

- The panel determines whether a thorough investigation of possible violations of the NCAA Constitution or bylaws has been conducted by the enforcement staff and/or the institution. If the panel determines that the investigation was inadequate, it must notify the enforcement staff and the parties and allow them to respond as appropriate.

- The panel may contact the institution, enforcement staff, and involved individuals for additional information or clarification prior to accepting or rejecting the proposed findings.

- If the agreed-upon findings and proposed penalties are approved, the panel prepares a report of its decision or adopts the written report of the parties. The panel may make additional comments explaining its analysis or amend the proposed findings, provided any addition or amendment is editorial and does not alter the substance of the findings. The written report may identify the chancellor or president of the institution (in cases involving lack of institutional control); the director of athletics and/or any individual with direct responsibility for and oversight of the athletics department (in cases involving lack of control and failure to monitor); the head coach(es) of the sport(s) involved; and, if appropriate, the chair or other members of the institution's governing body. The panel shall forward the report to the enforcement staff and the parties and publicly announce the resolution of the case.

- If the panel does not approve the findings, the case is processed through an infractions hearing, expedited hearing or on the written record.

- If the panel accepts the agreed-upon findings but proposes penalties in addition to those set forth in the parties' written report, the institution and/or involved individuals may accept those penalties or request an expedited hearing on penalties before the panel. The institution and/or involved individuals may appear before the panel in person, by video conference, or other mode of distance communication as the panel may deem appropriate to discuss the proposed additional penalties. The institution and/or involved individuals also may provide a written submission in lieu of a hearing. The panel may consider only information relevant to the imposition of penalties during the expedited hearing or, if no hearing is requested, on the written record. At the conclusion of the expedited hearing or review of the written record, the panel must prepare a written report and provide notification of its decision. The institution and/or any involved individuals may appeal additional penalties to the infractions appeals committee.

Expedited Hearing and Written Submissions (Level II Cases)

The institution or involved individual may petition the committee chair for an accelerated schedule for written submissions and an earlier hearing date (Bylaw 19.7.7.2). The petition shall be submitted not later than fourteen calendar days after the date of the notice of allegations. The enforcement staff may respond to the petition within five business days. The committee chair may grant or deny such a petition and set a reasonable schedule at his or her discretion.

Committee on Infractions Hearing (Level I and II Cases)

A panel of the Division I Committee on Infractions conducts hearings on Level I and II cases. The hearing panel will schedule an institution's hearing appearance in half-day or full-day blocks depending on the sophistication of its case.

Unless ordered by the committee chair, Level I and II cases "will be presented to and decided by hearing panels consisting of no less than five and no more than seven members of the full Committee on Infractions. Decisions issued by hearing panels are made on behalf of the Committee on Infractions" (Bylaw 19.3.3). Panels will be overseen by a chief hearing officer, who possesses the following authority:

- Consider and decide scheduling requests and extensions of time regarding hearing-related deadlines.
- For each hearing panel, appoint an individual responsible for conducting the press conference when the panel's decision is released.
- For each case set for hearing and in consultation with the committee chair, designate a panel member to serve as the committee appeals advocate for any appeal of the panel's decision.

- Coordinate with the office of the committee on infractions as necessary for logistic, administrative, or other support related to hearings to which the chief hearing officer is assigned.

A hearing panel will be assigned to the case. The panel "shall hold a hearing to make factual findings and to conclude whether violations of the NCAA Constitution and bylaws occurred and, if so, to prescribe appropriate penalties as set forth" in Bylaw 19.7.7. Further, the bylaw provides that an appearance by video conference or other distance communication may be available upon request "in cases that involve a small number of contested issues or cases in which the contested issues are relatively uncomplicated." The decision regarding the use of videoconferencing or other mode of communication "rests with the panel" (Bylaw 19.7.7). Further, in Level II cases, "the hearing will be conducted by telephone or videoconference unless an in-person hearing is requested by the panel, institution, enforcement staff or involved individual, or unless all participating parties agree to submit the case in writing without a hearing" (Bylaw 19.7.7).

Generally, the institution is represented at the hearing by its chief executive officer, faculty athletics representative, the director of athletics, the current or former head coach of the involved sport, compliance officer, legal counsel, or other pertinent individuals requested by the committee. The associate or assistant director of enforcement who conducted the investigation, the director of enforcement who supervised the processing of the case, and the vice president for enforcement services represent the enforcement staff at the hearing. Staff members who may have participated in some way in the processing of the case or who are present for other cases before the committee also may represent the enforcement staff at the hearing. The committee permits involved individuals appearing at a hearing to be present with legal counsel. The hearing is transcribed by a certified court reporter and tape-recorded by the committee.

The chief hearing officer opens the hearing by providing general background information concerning the hearing process. Next, the institution, the enforcement staff, and other involved individuals present opening statements. The enforcement staff follows with its presentation on the specifics of an allegation. The institution and other involved individuals make their presentations concerning the allegation at the conclusion of the enforcement staff's presentation. During this process, the hearing panel may ask questions of the enforcement staff, the institution, and other involved individuals. The next allegation is addressed only after the conclusion of a thorough discussion of the current allegation. After each allegation has been discussed, the enforcement staff, the institution, and other involved individuals provide closing statements.

The Infractions Report

After the hearing, the hearing panel deliberates in private and determines: (a) what findings should be made, if any; and (b) what penalties should be assessed, if any. The panel bases its decisions concerning violations on information deemed to be "credible, persuasive, and of a nature that reasonably prudent persons would rely upon in the conduct of serious affairs" (Bylaw 19.7.8.3). The panel prepares and approves a "final written infractions decision containing a statement of findings, conclusions, penalties, corrective actions, requirements and (for institutions) any other conditions and obligations of membership" (Bylaw 19.8.1). The committee on infractions releases the report approximately six to eight weeks after the hearing. The NCAA public affairs staff notifies the media of the infractions report on the morning of the release. However, the member institution and involved individuals obtain a copy of the report prior to the public release. A member designated by the chief hearing officer must conduct a press conference to announce the results of the committee's decision in each case. The committee also releases a public infractions report detailing the specific findings and penalties in the case, but with the names of all involved individuals redacted, on the day of the report's public release. Public infractions reports are posted on the NCAA website (http://www.ncaa.org). The committee does not comment on any case until it issues its infractions report.

Penalties

The committee can impose a variety of penalties, including, but not limited to, probationary periods, reduction of athletic scholarships, reduction of recruiting activities, and restrictions on a coach's athletically related duties. For violations that commenced before October 30, 2012, and continued after October 30, 2012, the hearing panel prescribes the penalties set forth in Bylaw 19.9.1 "unless it finds or concludes that the conduct constituting a violation predominately occurred before October 30, 2012." The panel will determine whether any factors present in a case may affect the imposition of penalties. The panel is required to "weigh any factors and determine whether a party should be subject to standard penalties or should be classified with aggravation or mitigation and, therefore, subject to a higher or lower range of penalties" (Bylaw 19.9.2). Bylaw 19.9.2 notes that "absent extenuating circumstances, core penalties corresponding to the classification shall be prescribed" as set forth in the current version of the NCAA Division I Manual.

Aggravated Case and Aggravating Factors

An aggravated case is one "where aggravating factors for a party outweigh mitigating factors for that party" (Bylaw 19.9.2.1). However, Bylaw 19.9.2.1 notes that "a case should not be classified as aggravated solely because the number of aggravating factors is larger than the number of mitigating factors" and that "an egregious aggravating factor may outweigh multiple mitigating factors." Aggravating factors are defined as "circumstances that warrant a higher range of penalties for a particular case" (Bylaw 19.9.3). The hearing panel is authorized to determine "whether aggravating factors are present in a case and the weight assigned to each factor" (Bylaw 19.9.3). Bylaw 19.9.3 provides examples of aggravating factors:

- Multiple Level I violations by the institution or an involved individual.
- A history of Level I, Level II, or major violations by the institution, sport program(s), or involved individual.
- Lack of institutional control.
- Obstructing an investigation or attempting to conceal the violation.
- Unethical conduct, compromising the integrity of an investigation, failing to cooperate during an investigation, or refusing to provide all relevant or requested information.
- Violations were premeditated, deliberate, or committed after substantial planning.

21

- Multiple Level II violations by the institution or an involved individual.
- Persons of authority condoned, participated in, or negligently disregarded the violation or related wrongful conduct.
- One or more violations caused significant ineligibility or other substantial harm to a student-athlete or prospective student-athlete.
- Conduct or circumstances demonstrating an abuse of a position of trust.
- A pattern of noncompliance within the sport program(s) involved.
- Conduct intended to generate pecuniary gain for the institution or involved individual.
- Intentional, willful, or blatant disregard for the NCAA Constitution or bylaws.
- Other facts warranting a higher penalty range.

Standard Case

A standard case is one "in which no mitigating or aggravating factors are present for a party or in which aggravating and mitigating factors for that party are generally of equal weight" (Bylaw 19.9.2.2). A standard case may warrant the standard range of penalties.

Mitigation Case and Mitigating Factors

A mitigation case is one "where mitigating factors outweigh aggravating factors" (Bylaw 19.9.2.3). Bylaw 19.9.2.3 notes "cases should not be classified as mitigated solely because the number of mitigating factors is larger than the number of aggravating factors." Mitigating factors are defined as "circumstances that warrant a lower range of penalties for a particular party" (Bylaw 19.9.4). The hearing panel is authorized to determine "whether mitigating factors are present in a case and the weight assigned to each factor" (Bylaw 19.9.4). Bylaw 19.9.4 provides examples of mitigating factors:

- Prompt self-detection and self-disclosure of the violation(s).
- Prompt acknowledgment of the violation, acceptance of responsibility, and (for an institution) imposition of meaningful corrective measures and/or penalties.

- Affirmative steps to expedite final resolution of the matter.
- An established history of self-reporting Level III or secondary violations.
- Implementation of a system of compliance methods designed to ensure rules compliance and satisfaction of institutional/coaches control standards.
- Exemplary cooperation.
- The violations were unintentional, limited in scope, and represent a deviation from otherwise compliant practices by the institution or involved individual.
- Other facts warranting a lower penalty range.

Appeals of Committee on Infractions Findings and Penalties

Institutions and involved individuals have the option to appeal the committee on infractions hearing panel's findings and penalties to the infractions appeals committee by filing a notice of appeal with the NCAA president "not later than 15 calendar days from the date of the public release of the committee's report" (Bylaw 19.10.2). Afterward, the appealing parties and the committee on infractions submit papers to the appeals committee. Next, the appeals committee conducts a hearing involving the appealing party and the committee on infractions representative. However, if the appealing party chooses to submit its appeal in writing only, the appeals committee considers the appeal based on the parties' written submissions without a hearing.

The infractions appeals committee can reverse or modify a finding of the committee on infractions hearing panel only if the institution or involved individual shows one or more of the following grounds (Bylaw 19.10.1.2):

- The committee on infractions hearing panel's finding is clearly contrary to the evidence presented to the hearing panel.
- The facts found by the committee on infractions hearing panel do not constitute a violation of the NCAA Constitution or bylaws.
- There was a procedural error, and but for the error, the committee on infractions hearing panel would not have made the finding of violation.

A penalty determined by the committee on infractions hearing panel, "including determinations regarding the existence and weighing of any aggravating or mitigating factors, shall not be set aside on appeal except on a showing by the appealing party that the panel abused its discretion" (Bylaw 19.10.1.1).

The procedure for processing an appeal is posted on the infractions appeals committee webpage, located on the NCAA website (http://www.ncaa.org).

After deliberating, the appeals committee issues its decision in an infraction appeals report. Public infraction appeals reports are posted on the NCAA website.

CHAPTER 3

DIVISIONS II AND III: THE NCAA ENFORCEMENT PROCESS

The NCAA enforcement process for Divisions II and III addresses instances wherein a member institution is in noncompliance with NCAA legislation. Some athletic conferences also have formal enforcement processes to review alleged violations of conference and NCAA rules. The enforcement process is designed to be a cooperative program involving member institutions, involved individuals, athletic conferences, and the NCAA enforcement staff to: (a) reduce secondary and major violations of NCAA legislation; and (b) impose appropriate corrective measures and penalties if violations occurred at an institution (Bylaw 19.01.1). A *secondary violation* is a violation that is "isolated or inadvertent in nature, provides or is intended to provide only a minimal recruiting, competitive or other advantage and does not include any significant recruiting inducement or extra benefit" (Bylaw 19.02.2.1). However, the NCAA can consider the occurrence of multiple secondary violations as a major violation (Bylaw 19.02.2.1). A *major violation* is a violation "other than secondary violations" and includes infractions "that provide an extensive recruiting or competitive advantage" (Bylaw 19.02.2.2).

Initiation of the Enforcement Process

The NCAA enforcement process is initiated in a number of ways. For example, the NCAA enforcement staff can initiate an investigation when it receives information or an allegation from a media report, an anonymous or a nonattributable source (e.g., high-school and college coaches, student-athletes, the general public) concerning a possible violation of NCAA legislation at a member institution (Bylaws 32.2.1 and 32.2.1.1; Enforcement/Infractions, 2004). In addition, enforcement staff investigations begin after a member institution discovers and self-reports violations to the staff (Bylaw 32.2.1.2). Finally, the enforcement staff makes "proactive efforts" to discover potential violations, including: (a) interviewing highly recruited prospective student-athletes and student-athletes who have transferred from member institutions; or (b) attending selected athletics contests and events (e.g., high-school or two-year college all-star games) that may be attended by college coaches (Enforcement/Infractions, 2004). When the enforcement staff receives allegations or other information concerning a possible violation of NCAA legislation, the information is evaluated by a director of major enforcement (Enforcement/ Infractions, 2004). If the information pertains to a secondary violation of NCAA legislation, the information may be provided to the member institution or the institution's athletic conference for review (Bylaws 32.2.2.1.3 and 32.4.1). If the information is deemed to be of a serious nature, however, it is assigned to an assistant director for a follow-up examination (Enforcement/Infractions, 2004).

The enforcement staff is permitted to start a review of a member institution only when the staff has "reasonable cause" to believe that the institution "may have violated NCAA legislation" (Enforcement/ Infractions, 2004). If this burden is satisfied, the staff determines whether the possible violation should be reviewed via correspondence with the involved member institution or its athletic conference or whether the enforcement staff should conduct its own in-person inquiries (Bylaw 32.2.2.1).

Notice of Inquiry and Investigation of Allegations

When the enforcement staff receives "reasonably reliable" information that "an intentional violation has occurred, that a significant competitive or recruiting advantage may have been gained, or that false or misleading information may have been reported to the member institution or to the enforcement staff," the staff begins to investigate the information to determine its credibility (Bylaw 32.5.1; Enforcement/Infractions, 2004).

At that time, the involved member institution is informed of the enforcement staff's investigation via a *notice of inquiry* to the institution's chief executive officer (Bylaw 32.5.1). The notice of inquiry also may indicate: (a) the involved sports; (b) the nature of the potential violations; (c) the approximate time period in which the alleged violations occurred; (d) the identities of the involved individuals; (e) the approximate time frame for the investigation; and (f) a statement that other facts may be developed during the investigation that may relate to additional violations (Bylaw 32.5.1). A notice of inquiry is not released to the public by the enforcement staff (Enforcement/Infractions, 2004). However, the member institution has the discretion to publicly release the notice (Enforcement/ Infractions, 2004).

During the investigation phase, the enforcement staff is required to notify the member institution of the status of its investigation within six months of the date after the notice of inquiry is received by the institution's chief executive officer (Bylaw 32.5.1.1). If the investigation continues, additional status reports must be provided to the institution at least every six months thereafter (Bylaw 32.5.1.1). If the enforcement staff determines that "there is sufficient information to warrant an allegation, it shall issue a cover letter and notice of allegations to the president or chancellor of the institution involved (with copies to the faculty athletics representative and the director of athletics and to the executive officer of the conference of which the institution is a member)" (Bylaw 32.6.1). However, if the enforcement staff believes that further evaluation is not needed, the staff will provide written notice of its decision to the institution (Bylaw 32.5.1; Enforcement/Infractions, 2004).

Notice of Allegations and Prehearing Procedures

The enforcement staff conducts investigations for a "reasonable period of time" to assess whether information exists that shows evidence of major violations of NCAA legislation (Enforcement/Infractions, 2004). If the staff determines that "sufficient information" exists to determine that a major violation occurred at a member institution, then a *notice of allegations* is sent to the institution's chief executive officer (Bylaw 32.6.1). The notice contains specific allegations of NCAA rules violations against an institution (Bylaw 32.6.1.1; Enforcement/Infractions, 2004). The enforcement staff also notifies athletic department personnel and student-athletes—whose employment or athletic eligibility could be affected—of the allegations in a notice of allegations in which they are named (Bylaw 32.6.1).

The institution and involved individuals have ninety days to respond to the notice of allegations (Bylaw 32.6.5). However, the institution and involved individuals may request additional time to respond (Bylaw 32.6.5). An institution is required to provide copies of pertinent portions of its response to "each involved individual in the case" (Bylaw 32.6.2). Involved individuals who have submitted a response are required to provide their response to the involved institutions and other involved individuals (Bylaw 32.6.2).

The enforcement staff establishes a secure site within thirty days of the date that the notice of allegations has been forwarded to the member institution (Bylaw 32.6.4). The site is required to provide a member institution or involved individual "reasonable access" to the enforcement staff's copies of tape-recorded interviews, interview summaries, interview transcripts, and other evidentiary information pertinent to an infractions case (Bylaw 32.6.4). The NCAA national office in Indianapolis, Indiana, or a location near the involved member institution or involved individual serves as a custodial site (Bylaw 32.6.4). The enforcement staff is required to inform the institution and involved individuals if information is developed subsequent to the thirty-day period (Bylaw 32.6.4.1). Any additions made to the information after the thirty-day period are sent directly to the institution and involved individuals (Bylaw 32.6.4.1).

After the institution and the involved individuals respond to the enforcement staff's allegations, a hearing date is set before the committee on infractions (Enforcement/Infractions 2004). The enforcement staff conducts separate prehearing conferences with the institution and involved individuals after the institution's submission of its written response to the notice of allegations (Bylaw 32.6.6). During the prehearing conference, the enforcement staff, the institution, and involved individuals confer on issues and questions concerning the allegations (Bylaw 32.6.6).

The enforcement staff prepares a document called the *enforcement staff case summary* prior to the hearing (Bylaw 32.6.7). The case summary lists the allegations, the position of the institution and involved individuals on each allegation, any remaining issues, the identity of individuals involved in the case, and any other pertinent information (Bylaw 32.6.7). The case summary is provided to the institution, involved individuals, and the committee on infractions no later than two weeks prior to the hearing date (Bylaw 32.6.7; Enforcement/Infractions, 2004).

As an alternative, eligible member institutions and involved individuals may elect to process a major infractions case through *summary disposition*, a procedure used in place of a formal committee hearing. Summary disposition requires the NCAA enforcement staff, the member institution, and involved individuals to agree with the facts of a case and stipulate that the facts constitute major violations of NCAA legislation (Bylaw 32.7.1). The member institution and involved individuals also propose penalties that address the stipulated violations (Bylaw 32.7.1.3). The committee on infractions has the authority to: (a) approve the agreed-upon findings and proposed penalties; (b) not approve the findings (which will result in a hearing); (c) not approve the proposed penalties (which can result in an expedited hearing); or (d) request additional information (Bylaws 32.7.1.4.1, 32.7.1.4.2, 32.7.1.4.3, and 32.7.1.4.4).

Committee on Infractions Hearing and Infractions Report

The Division I Committee on Infractions meets several times per year (the Divisions II and III committees meet less frequently; NCAA Enforcement Services Group, 2004). A committee meeting typically lasts two to three days and is often held during a weekend (NCAA Enforcement Services Group, 2004). The number of institutions appearing at a hearing during a committee meeting depends on the length of each case as well as other items on the committee's agenda (NCAA Enforcement Services Group, 2004). The committee generally schedules an institution's hearing appearance in half-day or full-day blocks depending on the sophistication of its case (NCAA Enforcement Services Group, 2004; Committees on Infractions, 2003, 3).

Generally, the institution is represented at the hearing by its president or chancellor, the institution's director of athletics, the current or former head coach of the involved sport, the compliance officer, legal counsel, enrolled student-athletes whose eligibility could be affected by information presented at the hearing, or other pertinent individuals requested by the committee (Bylaw 32.8.6.2). The assistant director of enforcement who conducted the investigation, the director of enforcement who supervised the processing of the case, and the vice president for enforcement services represent the enforcement staff at the hearing (NCAA Enforcement Services Group, 2004; Committees on Infractions, 2003, 1–4). Staff members who may have participated in some way in the processing of the case or who are present for other cases before the committee also may represent the enforcement staff at the hearing (NCAA Enforcement Services Group, 2004). The committee permits involved individuals appearing at a hearing to be present with legal counsel (Bylaw 32.8.6.1). The hearing is transcribed by a certified court reporter and tape-recorded by the committee (Bylaw 32.8.7.7; Committees on Infractions, 2003, 4).

The chair of the committee opens the hearing by providing general background information concerning the hearing process (Committees on Infractions, 2003, 1–2). Next, the institution, the enforcement staff, and other involved individuals present opening statements (Bylaw 32.8.7.1). The enforcement staff follows with its presentation on the specifics of an allegation (Bylaw 32.8.7.2). The institution and other involved individuals make their presentations concerning the allegation at the conclusion of the enforcement staff's presentation (Bylaw 32.8.7.3). During this process, the committee may ask questions of the enforcement staff, the institution, and other involved individuals (Bylaw 32.8.7.6). The next allegation is addressed only after a thorough discussion of the current allegation. After each allegation has been discussed, the enforcement staff, the institution, and involved individuals provide closing statements (Bylaw 32.8.7.1).

After the hearing, the committee deliberates in private and determines: (a) what findings should be made, if any; and (b) what penalties should be assessed, if any (Bylaw 32.8.8). The committee bases its decisions concerning violations on information deemed to be "credible, persuasive, and of a kind on which reasonably prudent persons rely in the conduct of serious affairs" (Bylaw 32.8.8.2). The committee can impose a variety of penalties, including, but not limited to, probationary periods, reduction of athletic scholarships, reduction of recruiting activities, and restrictions on a coach's athletically related duties (Bylaw 19.5.2).

The committee's decision is framed in an *infractions report.* A member of the committee is assigned to write the report (Enforcement/Infractions, 2004). The report outlines the findings made and penalties imposed by the committee as well as the rationale for the committee's decisions (Bylaw 32.9.1). The committee releases the infractions report approximately six to eight weeks after the hearing (Enforcement/Infractions, 2004). The NCAA public affairs staff notifies the media of the report on the morning of the release (Bylaw 32.9.2; Enforcement/Infractions, 2004). However, the member institution and involved individuals obtain a copy of the report the day prior to the public release (Enforcement/Infractions, 2004). The committee chair (or other designated committee member) conducts a press conference to announce the results of the committee's decision in each case (Bylaw 32.9.2.2). The committee also releases a public infractions report detailing the findings and penalties in the case, but with the names of all involved individuals redacted, on the day of the report's public release (Enforcement/Infractions, 2004). Public infractions reports are posted on the NCAA website (http://www.ncaa.org). The committee does not comment on any case until it issues its infractions report (Enforcement/ Infractions, 2004).

Appeals of Committee on Infractions Findings and Penalties

Institutions and involved individuals have the option to appeal the committee on infractions' findings and penalties to division-specific appeals committees by filing a notice of appeal with the NCAA president "not later than 15 calendar days from the date of the public release of the Committee on Infractions' public infractions decision" (Bylaw 32.10.1). Afterward, the appealing parties and the committee on infractions submit papers to the appeals committee (Bylaw 32.10.2). Next, the appeals committee conducts a hearing involving the appealing party and the committee on infractions representative (Bylaw 32.11.1). However, if the appealing party chooses to submit its appeal in writing only, the appeals committee considers the appeal based on the parties' written submissions without a hearing (Bylaws 32.10.1 and 32.10.1.1).

An appeals committee can reverse or modify a ruling of the committee on infractions only if the institution or involved individual shows one or more of the following grounds:

- The committee on infractions' ruling was clearly contrary to the evidence.
- The institution's or involved individual's actions did not constitute a violation of NCAA legislation.
- A procedural ruling significantly affected the reliability of the information that was used to support the committee on infractions' findings.
- The penalty assessed was excessive or inappropriate (Bylaws 32.10.4.1 and 32.10.4.2).

After deliberating, the appeals committee issues its decision in an *infraction appeals report* (Bylaw 32.9.1). Public infraction appeals reports are posted on the NCAA website (http://www.ncaa.org).

PART 2

INTERNAL INVESTIGATIONS

CHAPTER 1

PURPOSE AND START OF AN INTERNAL INVESTIGATION

Internal investigations that address allegations of NCAA rule violations present challenges to any NCAA member institution or involved individual. In particular, college administrators must make difficult decisions when allegations implicating the athletic program surface, including whether to conduct an internal investigation and how to perform one (Marshall 1999; Kuehne 1997, 653). Moreover, the mere allegation of wrongdoing in an athletic program creates an atmosphere of scandal and crisis throughout the institution and its community (Kuehne 1997, 653). Increasingly, institutions are finding that the negative effects of the NCAA enforcement process can be lessened if they conduct a thorough and effective internal investigation. This chapter describes strategies and techniques that can be applied when an institution conducts an internal investigation on its own initiative or performs a joint inquiry with the NCAA enforcement staff.

Purpose of an Internal Investigation into an Athletic Program

Institutions conducting internal investigations in intercollegiate athletic programs are confronted with numerous challenges, time-consuming obligations, and public scrutiny. In addition, the methodology used by an institution to conduct an internal investigation influences how it responds to a notice of allegations or prepares for an infractions hearing. As a result, an internal investigation must focus on the collection of information that addresses: (a) what the facts are; (b) what persons and organizations were involved in the alleged violation of NCAA legislation; (c) why the alleged violation occurred; (d) what corrective measures and self-imposed penalties are needed to address the situation; and (e) what institution policies and procedures are relevant to the alleged violation (Buckner 2002; Marshall 1999).

First, an institution is able to fulfill its procedural obligations with a well-planned internal investigation. Specifically, an investigation should uncover: (a) whether the institution is required to disclose certain information to the NCAA or its athletic conference; (b) whether the institution is required to implement corrective measures and self-imposed penalties to address any identified deficiencies in its policies, procedures, and processes; and (c) whether the institution has documented policies or procedures designed to prevent the alleged violations of NCAA legislation, and, if so, whether an institutional employee, student-athlete, or athletic representative failed to follow the policies or procedures at issue (Buckner 2002; Marshall 1999).

Second, an internal investigation should identify the persons and organizations involved in the alleged violations. In particular, the institution must identify: (a) who was involved in the alleged wrongdoing; (b) who possesses information pertinent to the investigation; and (c) who has been interviewed by the NCAA enforcement staff and athletic conference officials (Buckner 2002; Marshall 1999). In addition, the institution's investigation should ascertain whether institutional administrators, employees, student-athletes, and athletic representatives are individually liable under NCAA legislation (Buckner 2002; Marshall 1999).

Third, an internal investigation should discover why the alleged violation of NCAA legislation occurred as well as the level of intent of the person or persons who committed the violation (Buckner 2002; Marshall 1999).

The Start of an Internal Investigation

An institution can conduct an effective internal investigation only if its administrators, trustees, and regents understand the purposes for initiating an investigation. In addition, productive inquiries occur at institutions whose administrators, trustees, and regents recognize: (a) the legal and NCAA enforcement issues that may be considered during the process; and (b) how those issues will influence campus policy and life for a number of years (Buckner 2002; Marshall 1999).

An institution should start the internal investigation process when campus or athletic administrators receive a credible allegation of wrongdoing involving the athletic program. Allegations of wrongdoing involving NCAA legislation can come from various sources, including: (a) complaints, tips, or anonymous reports; (b) NCAA, athletic conference, government agency, or auditor reports that identify suspect practices concerning NCAA legislation; (c) requests for information or documents from the NCAA, athletic conference, or government agency; and (d) criminal or civil proceedings in the state or federal court systems (Buckner 2002; Marshall 1999).

If an institution declines to review the substance of an allegation, it risks creating a scenario where the NCAA, its athletic conference, or another entity (e.g., media) learns of the institution's failure to investigate the allegation. Furthermore, an institution that chooses to begin an internal investigation after the NCAA issues a notice of inquiry or notice of allegations sacrifices the strategic advantages and opportunities (e.g., conducting interviews before any other party; implementing an offensive public relations strategy) it possesses in the early stages of an inquiry (Buckner 2002; Marshall 1999).

An institution also may face other consequences associated with conducting an internal investigation. For example, the institution may be required to disclose the results of its internal investigation to the NCAA enforcement staff and athletic conference officials. In fact, NCAA Bylaws 32.1.4 and 19.01.3 require all member institutions to cooperate fully with the NCAA enforcement staff and the committees on infractions. Furthermore, the internal investigation may provide an opportunity for disgruntled student-athletes or employees to file civil lawsuits for claims or to report further allegations of NCAA or criminal violations. In addition, the internal investigation, even if it is conducted with professionalism, skill, and care, can be intrusive and unsettling throughout the institution and local community (Marshall 1999). Finally, the internal investigation may identify major violations of NCAA legislation that the enforcement staff may not have discovered during the enforcement and conference staffs' inquiry.

Nevertheless, an institution faces less of a risk when it conducts an internal investigation than it does when failing to take allegations, rumors, or the NCAA enforcement process seriously.

CHAPTER 2

ORGANIZING AND PLANNING THE INTERNAL INVESTIGATION

Choosing the Internal Investigator: General Counsel, Special Investigative Committee, Outside Attorney, or Private Investigator?

An institution conducting an internal investigation must decide who should conduct it. The institution can appoint its in-house legal counsel (general counsel) or a *special investigative committee*. A special investigative committee, which is composed of administrators, faculty members, staff, and other persons with relevant expertise, is created to probe alleged violations of NCAA legislation and institutional rules and regulations in an athletic program. A special investigative committee also refers to a body composed of noninstitutional personnel and experts who are appointed by an institution's chief executive officer or an elected official to investigate alleged violations of federal and state law, institutional rules and regulations, and/or NCAA legislation in an athletic program. Alternatively, the institution can retain outside legal counsel or a licensed private investigator with NCAA enforcement experience to conduct the inquiry. (For the purposes of this book, the person or committee conducting an inquiry on behalf of an institution will be referred to as an internal investigator.)

However, at a minimum, the institution should consider appointing or retaining an attorney to supervise the internal investigation. This strategy preserves the confidentiality of the legal questions and sensitive issues that may arise during the inquiry (Marsh and Robbins 2003, 684; Marshall 1999). Specifically, if an attorney is conducting or supervising the investigation, the institution can shield confidential and sensitive information by asserting the *attorney-client privilege* and/or *work-product doctrine* (Marshall 1999). The attorney-client privilege allows a client "to refuse to disclose and to prevent any other person from disclosing confidential communications" (*Black's Law Dictionary*, 6th ed., s.v. "attorney-client privilege") between the client and the client's attorney. The work-product doctrine protects notes, working documents, memoranda, or other materials prepared by "an attorney in anticipation of litigation" (*Black's Law Dictionary*, 6th ed., s.v. "work product rule"). An investigator should review the open-records or sunshine laws in the institution's state to assess if they contain an exemption for documents protected by a legal privilege (Marsh and Robbins 2003, 686). This review will influence the procedures an institution uses for the release of investigative materials requested under open-records or sunshine laws (Marsh and Robbins 2003, 687).

The appointment of an institution's general counsel or special investigative committee to lead an internal investigation can provide numerous benefits. For example, general counsel or committee members can be more compelling in promoting the benefits of investigating alleged violations of NCAA legislation (Marshall 1999). Furthermore, general counsel or committee members are familiar with the institution's culture, organizational structure, policies, procedures, operations, and personnel (Marshall 1999). As a result, general counsel or committee members are able to obtain greater assistance from institutional personnel in responding to investigation-related requests (e.g., interviews, information, documents) from the NCAA enforcement staff and athletic conference officials. Finally, general counsel or committee members' appointments can reduce investigation costs since outside counsel or private investigators would not be retained to conduct the inquiry (Marshall 1999).

Despite the advantages of general counsel or special investigative committee appointments, the institution is well served to retain experienced outside legal counsel or a licensed private investigator in most situations. In fact, an institution benefits from outside experts who have: (a) the capacity to be impartial in evaluating the institution's policies and procedures; (b) an investigation background or experience in the NCAA enforcement process; (c) the ability to draw on established credibility with the NCAA enforcement staff; and (d) sufficient staff and resources to conduct an investigation efficiently (Marsh and Robbins 2003, 683–84; Buckner 2002; Marshall 1999).

An institution benefits in other ways from retaining outside counsel or a private investigator to conduct an internal investigation. For instance, the institution, its general counsel, or members of the special investigative committee may not possess the infrastructure, time, or resources to conduct an internal investigation (Marsh and Robbins 2003, 683–84; Marshall 1999). Also, even if the general counsel or committee members possess sufficient time and resources, it may be improper or impractical for the institution to divert appointed personnel from other academic, legal, or administrative commitments during a multiyear investigation (Marshall 1999).

Furthermore, it is more difficult to assert and maintain the attorney-client privilege when an institution's general counsel or a special investigative committee conducts an internal investigation (Marshall 1999). For instance, a general counsel is frequently requested to provide institutions with business and legal advice concerning the issues under investigation as part of his or her normal duties as an employee of the institution (Marshall 1999). Thus the law in many states precludes organizations from applying the attorney-client privilege to communications between the organization and a general counsel in his or her role as an employee. Also, an institution lacks the ability to assert a privilege over a special investigative committee's work because the presence of an attorney-client relationship cannot be established between the institution and the committee.

Finally, an institution benefits from not placing general counsel or members of special investigative committees in the position of making difficult decisions regarding an investigation, including: (a) issues concerning employee matters (e.g., termination, suspension); (b) content of disclosures to the NCAA enforcement staff or athletic conference officials; and (c) explanation of how and why violations of NCAA legislation occurred at the institution (Marshall 1999).

Overall, an effective internal investigation, which protects the privileged and confidential status of investigative materials, can be conducted using one of two organizational structures. One option involves an investigation conducted by outside counsel or a private investigator under the supervision of the institution's general counsel or a special investigative committee. This organizational structure provides an institution with the best of both worlds: (a) the general counsel's or committee members' knowledge of the institution; and (b) the outside counsel's or private investigator's in-depth experience in the NCAA enforcement process (Buckner 2002; Marshall 1999).

Alternatively, the privilege and confidential status of information produced during an internal investigation can be maintained if the internal investigator is hired by outside legal counsel. In this organizational structure, the internal investigator reports to the institution through the outside counsel. This arrangement acknowledges established law that applies the attorney-client privilege to communications involving "experts," such as internal investigators, when: (a) the investigator is working under the direction and supervision of legal counsel; and (b) the investigator's advice is not revealed to persons outside those in the institution with a need to know (Marshall 1999). In this reporting structure, communication between internal investigators and outside counsel should be marked "confidential" and "privileged." If the institution chooses to organize the reporting scheme in this way, the retention/engagement agreement between the internal investigator and outside counsel should address this issue (Marshall 1999).

Planning the Investigation

Once the institution determines who will lead the internal investigation, it is crucial to properly plan the inquiry. The planning phase involves: (a) reaching a preliminary determination of the scope, goals, facts, and issues involved in the inquiry; and (b) preparing the investigation plan and chart.

Preliminary Determination

An institution and the internal investigator should begin planning the internal investigation by making a *preliminary determination* of the following items (Buckner 2002; Poteet 2001, 13–15; Marshall 1999; Kuehne 1997, 666–68; Lynch and Fuchs 1996, 623–24):

- Legal and factual issues expected to be encountered during the investigation.
- Potential legal exposure and NCAA sanctions faced by the institution.
- Location, volume, and identity of the key documents to be reviewed.
- Identity and location of key persons to be interviewed.
- Coordination of the communication of the institution's investigation with the NCAA enforcement staff and athletic conference officials.
- Organization of the reporting and supervising scheme for the internal investigation.

- Contingency measures.
- Identity of additional persons, experts, or groups to assist the internal investigator.

The final aspect of the preliminary determination discussion involves the institution and the internal investigator agreeing on the scope and goals of the internal investigation. If the institution understands the focus of an ongoing NCAA enforcement staff inquiry when it begins an internal investigation, the institution's investigation should be consistent with the NCAA inquiry (Buckner 2002; Marshall 1999; Kuehne 1997, 666). Conversely, if the institution's internal investigation was initiated by allegations of infractions not originally reported to the NCAA, the investigator should plan and conduct a comprehensive, but focused, investigation. Such an investigation allows an institution to understand the complete scope of its exposure under NCAA legislation and to fulfill its membership obligations.

Investigation Plan

After a preliminary determination has been reached between the institution and the internal investigator, the investigator should prepare an *investigation plan* and *investigation chart* (Buckner 2002; Kuehne 1997, 666). An investigation plan maps out the strategy and steps involved in an inquiry and includes, at a minimum, the following items:

- Documentation of the conclusions reached during the preliminary determination.
- Issues, topics, and matters to be examined during the investigation.
- A detailed investigative task list, including: (a) identification of responsibilities for each investigation team member; and (b) estimate of the time line (i.e., anticipated start and completion dates) for each investigative task.
- The plan and procedure for client-investigator communication.
- Identification of staff, areas, offices, and departments that will be involved in the investigation.
- Identification of additional expertise or logistical support required by the investigator.

- Expected fees and costs.
- Milestones and report dates.
- Possible outcomes.

The plan should be reviewed and approved by the institution's chief executive officer or the person at the institution to whom the investigator reports. After the plan has been approved, the internal investigator should review the plan periodically during the inquiry. Most important, the plan should be flexible so that it can be revised if the internal investigator receives pertinent additional information or feedback, including: (a) addition of tasks to address any oversights; (b) adjustments to the investigation time line; (c) determination if additional documents must be collected or persons interviewed; and (d) identification of issues or allegations that require a separate investigation (Kuehne 1997, 666).

Based on the available information, an investigator prepares an initial investigation chart. The chart contains the associations of people and organizations (Kinnee 1994, 79–80), as well as important events, involved in the alleged violation. This exercise enables an investigator to understand the assorted information in a visual format (Kinnee 1994, 79). Also, an investigation chart can be used to prepare for interviews or to design evidence searches. The chart should be revised as the investigator collects additional information (Kinnee 1994, 79).

Investigation Management File

An effective investigation is maintained through the documentation, filing, and maintenance of information collected by investigators. A well-organized investigation management file allows investigators to quickly and efficiently access or locate the log of collected physical evidence, interview tapes, and summaries, the list of important persons and organizations, the resource directory, and other investigative materials (Nicholson 2000, 12–15, 64). An investigation management file consists of the following elements: (a) a means to catalog the information, using a computer system, filing system, or card reference system; and (b) a secure place to store the information (Nicholson 2000, 12, 64–65). No matter what system an investigator implements, however, it must be organized, maintained, and able to provide the investigator with information at a moment's notice. Most important, a complete investigation management file puts in one place everything that assists the investigator when preparing the institution's self-report, its response to the notice of allegations, and its infractions hearing presentation.

CHAPTER 3

CONDUCTING THE INVESTIGATION

An internal investigation consists of the following elements: (a) communication; (b) analysis of documents, files, and other physical evidence; and (c) interviews.

Communication

The first element of an internal investigation involves the communication of the internal investigator's role to affected personnel at the institution, NCAA enforcement staff, and athletic conference officials. Specifically, the institution should inform senior institutional administrators, the NCAA director and/or assistant director of major enforcement assigned to the case, and the conference commissioner that an internal investigator has been retained to furnish legal and/or investigative advice. The internal investigator also should contact the NCAA enforcement staff and athletic conference officials during this period. This communication can be a first step in constructing a relationship that facilitates open communication throughout the process (Buckner 2002; Marshall 1999).

In addition, the agreement between the internal investigator and the institution should include specific language on the institution's engagement of the investigator. Furthermore, if the confidentiality of the investigation is not in contention, institutions can distribute a memorandum to institutional personnel, students, and representatives prior to the start of the interview process (Marshall 1999; Kuehne 1997, 665). The memorandum's purpose would be to inform the campus community of the internal investigation and to request the community's cooperation with investigators (Marshall 1999; Kuehne 1997, 665). This type of notification reduces rumors, suspicion, speculation, and stress on campus (Marshall 1999; Kuehne 1997, 665).

The institution and internal investigator must be careful about how they communicate with each other. In particular, all communication between the internal investigator and the institution (including personnel and student-athletes) must remain confidential. A procedure should be implemented to separate privileged and confidential written communications from other documents. Privileged and confidential documents should be clearly marked in accordance with such classifications (Buckner 2002; Marshall 1999).

If the internal investigator is not an attorney, oral exchanges can be used to communicate information that does not fit within the attorney-client privilege, work-product doctrine, or other confidential classification under state or federal law. Thus it is important for the institution to clearly identify the person (e.g., counsel, senior administrator) or group (e.g., special investigative committee) to whom the internal investigator reports so that all parties can prevent the improper disclosure of confidential or privileged information (Buckner 2002; Marshall 1999). As discussed in an earlier chapter, the privileged and confidential status of information produced during an internal investigation also can be maintained if the internal investigator is hired by outside legal counsel.

Analysis of Documents, Files, and Other Physical Evidence

The collection of documents, files, and other physical evidence relevant to an inquiry is one of the most important tasks during an internal investigation. An internal investigator's level of success in this area can help determine the effectiveness of interviews as well as the outcome of the investigation.

Evidence Collection Considerations

When an institution is conducting an internal investigation or cooperating with the NCAA enforcement staff in a joint inquiry, the collection of documents, files, and other physical evidence requires balancing competing concerns. In particular, the institution's document collection and submission activities should be carefully formulated to minimize the risk of a waiver of a privilege (Buckner 2002; Marshall 1999; Kuehne 1997, 678–79). On the other hand, the institution should be careful not to withhold any information requested by the NCAA enforcement staff under NCAA legislation. Specifically, NCAA Bylaws 10.1, 19, and 32 prohibit concealment, destruction, alteration, or fabrication of documents or other information during the enforcement process.

An investigator's collection of documents, files, and other physical evidence should be well-planned and structured to obtain reliable evidence. The collection and documentation of evidence in criminal investigations are generally performed by law enforcement agencies that rely on proven techniques (Nicholson 2000, 37). Law enforcement personnel use evidence to locate and identify witnesses, establish a party's mode of operation, "proving or disproving an alibi, and connecting or eliminating suspects" (Nicholson 2000, 37). It is advisable for an internal investigator conducting an inquiry in the NCAA enforcement process to apply these techniques, some of which are summarized later in this chapter. This will guarantee that the evidence collected: (a) can be used to construct the institution's theory of the case; and (b) will be admissible in a committee on infractions hearing.

Evidence collected during an investigation can be used for varying purposes and in different venues. It is important for an investigator to keep this in mind when evidence is found or collected. For instance, an investigator should contact law enforcement to gather evidence that may be linked to criminal activity, including illegal objects, drugs, and weapons (Nicholson 2000, 38). Furthermore, evidence collected for use in the NCAA enforcement process should be marked and maintained in a secure area to maintain the *chain of custody*.

The chain of custody applies to the handling of evidence in an investigation. Because evidence collected during an investigation can be used by an institution and involved individuals in an infractions hearing to support or deny allegations, it must be handled in a deliberate manner to avoid claims of inauthenticity, tampering, or misconduct (Evans and Stagner 2003, 563; Patzakis 2003, 1–3). Thus the institution and involved individuals must designate a person to maintain physical custody of a piece(s) of evidence (Evans and Stagner 2003, 563; Patzakis 2003, 1–3). The chain of custody is established when the investigator collects a piece of evidence, documents its collection, and stores it in a secure place (Evans and Stagner 2003, 563; Patzakis 2003, 1–3). Chain of custody is maintained when every activity between the collection of evidence and its appearance at an infractions hearing is completely documented (Evans and Stagner 2003, 563; Patzakis 2003, 1–3).

Evidence Collection Guidelines

An internal investigator should use a five-step methodology to collect evidence.

First, an institution should review, and possibly suspend, its document destruction policy at the initiation of an internal investigation or when it has reason to believe a violation of NCAA legislation occurred (Boese 2002, 2, 4). At the very least, the institution should notify personnel in writing that potentially relevant documents are not to be destroyed until after an investigator determines their relevance (Boese 2002, 6). Also, an institution must advise its employees, student-athletes, and athletic representatives to maintain relevant documents in a secure location (ideally as maintained in the normal course of business) until the documents can be gathered and reviewed by an investigator (Boese 2002, 4). The institution should also remind employees, student-athletes, and athletic representatives that altering, destroying, concealing, or fabricating documents during the investigative process is a violation of institutional rules and NCAA legislation (Boese 2002, 6). Finally, the communication should inform persons that documents include electronic mail, CD-ROMs, DVDs, compact discs, and other electronic information systems (Boese 2002, 6).

Second, it is beneficial for an institution to appoint an institutional official as a *document custodian* and an *electronic document custodian* at the outset of an investigation. It is best to choose persons who are not involved or implicated in the allegations. The custodial appointments should be made in writing and provide the custodians with the necessary authority to gather evidence from the highest level in the institution (Boese 2002, 5–7).

The document custodian's duties include: (a) directing employees, students, and athletic representatives to search for and deliver (or inform the custodian of the location of) the requested documents and files; and (b) serving as a contact point inside the institution to coordinate these efforts (Boese 2002, 5–7). Ideally, the electronic document custodian should be an employee from the institution's IT department (Boese 2002, 5–7). The electronic document custodian's duties consist of searching, or, with the assistance of the investigator, retaining a qualified expert to search, smartphones, handheld computers, computers, data storage devices (e.g., USB flash drive), and other electronic files owned and operated by the institution for relevant materials (Boese 2002, 5–7). Some of the technical aspects of the electronic document custodian's duties can be outsourced to firms that specialize in computer forensic analysis. In conjunction with these appointments, an internal investigator should review the institution's automatic electronic mail deletion program, which could result in the deletion of relevant materials (Boese 2002, 5–7).

Third, the investigator conducts searches throughout the institution in offices and locations where an internal investigator and custodian reasonably believe relevant documents and files may be located. In addition, the investigator and custodian send written search requests for evidence to institutional personnel, student-athletes, and athletic representatives.

A few issues should be considered when conducting evidence searches. To begin with, the investigator should coordinate and schedule all evidence searches with the appropriate institutional officials. Also, investigators and custodians should consult the institution's legal counsel on the consequences of accessing stored electronic communications on a server under the federal Electronic Communications and Privacy Act (Clark and Diliberto 1996, 51). The law prohibits seizing and/or searching a computer, including electronic mail, of parties not involved in a crime or other illicit activities (Clark and Diliberto 1996, 51). Finally, custodians should document confirmations from institutional personnel and other parties that "an appropriate search has been conducted and that all responsive documents have been produced" (Boese 2002, 6–7). Custodians should also note if no relevant documents were found after a particular search request (Boese 2002, 6–7). This documentation should be drafted with the expectation that it could be submitted to the NCAA enforcement staff (Boese 2002, 6–7).

Fourth, an investigator or custodian collects and records the evidence. Generally, if evidence consists of a document or computer file, the investigator or custodian should make a copy of it and store the original in a secure location. Other physical evidence should be collected and properly stored in a secure location. Evidence of a sensitive nature (which will be discussed below) that will be submitted to an outside expert or a laboratory for analysis should be placed in an evidence bag and stored in a secure location. Local law enforcement agencies should be contacted to collect evidence relevant to the commission of a crime.

All evidence should be marked with a Bates stamp, a document number, or some other form of identification, with identification marks for sensitive evidence placed on the evidence bag. The information should include: (a) time and date that the document was processed as evidence;

(b) name of the investigator; (c) name of the person who produced or possessed the evidence; and (d) location of the evidence (Boese 2002, 7; Nicholson 2000, 38; Lynch and Fuchs 1996, 626–27). This information is recorded in a list called an *evidence log*, which is placed in the investigation management file (Nicholson 2000, 38).

If handwriting or typewriting on a collected document is at issue in the case, it is important to obtain sufficient writing samples for comparison with the collected document (FTDC 1993). Typical writing samples include documents prepared in normal transactions, including receipts, class notes, employment applications, letters, and fingerprint card signatures (FTDC 1993). Writing samples that share the date of the collected document are the best pieces for comparison (FTDC 1993). Samples also can be obtained during a person's interview (FTDC 1993). When collecting writing samples from an interview subject or other person(s), an investigator should mimic the conditions, if known, surrounding the preparation of the collected document, including using the same paper stock and style, document size, ink, writing instrument (e.g., pen, typewriter), writing style (e.g., handwriting, block lettering), and any other relevant medium (FTDC 1993). The collected evidence and writing samples should not be marked, defaced, or altered (FTDC 1993).

Evidence collected that can provide information leading to the discovery of further evidence, including whether a person handled a document or used a particular item, is *sensitive evidence*. For example, in a hypothetical case, the crucial issue is whether a head coach intentionally violated an NCAA bylaw one day after receiving a memorandum providing clear and unambiguous instructions on how not to violate the rule. In an interview, the coach declares that he did not receive and had no knowledge of information contained in the memorandum. If an evidence search uncovers a copy of the memorandum addressed to the coach, a trained investigator can dust the document for the coach's fingerprints. The presence of the coach's fingerprints on the memorandum would allow an investigator to reasonably conclude that the coach handled the document and lied about not receiving it. Sensitive evidence must be handled carefully by investigators and custodians. As previously explained, sensitive evidence is protected by being placed in an evidence bag before it is analyzed or reviewed.

Fifth, the investigator identifies, collects, and records additional evidence developed through further questioning of persons and an analysis of existing evidence (Nicholson 2000, 38–39). Investigators can identify and locate additional evidence relevant to the case after interviewing persons who produced or possessed the existing evidence. These persons may know where similar evidence may be found or know of other persons who have relevant information. In addition, investigators can uncover leads to new information after analyzing collected evidence.

Responding to a Request for Documents by the NCAA Enforcement Staff

When the NCAA enforcement staff submits a request for documents, it may be helpful for the institution to meet with the staff to determine the proper scope of the request as well as to clarify any ambiguities. The institution should document its discussion with the enforcement staff, including any clarifications involving the document request. Further, this discussion should be confirmed in writing via a letter or an electronic mail to the staff (Boese 2002, 5).

The institution has the right to review every relevant document to determine whether a privilege applies before submission to the NCAA (Boese 2002, 7; Clark 1999, 1; Lynch and Fuchs 1996, 626). If the institution withholds the production of any documents because of a privilege, a *privilege log* should be submitted with the documents that are produced to the NCAA (Boese 2002, 7; Clark 1999, 2). A privilege log describes the documents withheld from production without including the privileged language from the document (Clark 1999, 2). A typical privilege log contains the following information for each document (Clark 1999, 2):

- The Bates stamp or document number assigned to the document.
- The date of the document.
- The type of document (e.g., letter, memorandum, report).
- The author of the document.
- The recipient(s) of the document, including persons who received carbon copies (cc) and blind carbon copies (bcc).
- The type of privilege claimed (e.g., attorney-client, attorney work-product, self-evaluative privilege).

If an institution is responding to a document request, copies (not the originals) of documents should be produced along with a written cover letter listing the documents produced (Boese 2002, 7; Lynch and Fuchs 1996, 627). This technique avoids any disputes between the institution and the NCAA enforcement staff concerning what was and what was not produced to the staff (Boese 2002, 7). The cover letter should be approved in advance by the appropriate institutional administrator and the relevant document custodian (Boese 2002, 7). The institution should provide the enforcement staff with reasonable access to inspect and review other collected physical evidence.

Document Review and Analysis

As documents are collected, a prepared internal investigator conducts a systematic review and analysis of the information. This practice provides an investigator with a current assessment of the investigation and produces sources of new evidence. Also, it is preferable to review relevant documents (e.g., institutional forms, computer files, phone records, receipts) before conducting interviews because (Buckner 2002; Nicholson 2000, 65–91; Marshall 1999; Kuehne 1997, 678–79):

- Documents may identify persons who should be placed on the interview list. If necessary, an investigator can perform a background check (also referred to as a background investigation) on a person to acquire sufficient contact information or to provide other information necessary to complete the investigation. Background information should be obtained from reliable and consistent sources, including government agencies, legal records, directories, reference manuals, and reputable Internet sites. An institution can also outsource this work to an experienced private investigation firm.
- Documents can uncover critical issues and questions that can be answered only through interviews.
- Documents can be used to refresh the memories of persons during interviews.

Interviews

Interview Subjects

The third element in an internal investigation involves conducting interviews. At a minimum, the internal investigator should interview the following individuals: (a) person or persons who made the allegation or complaint; (b) person or persons who allegedly violated NCAA legislation; (c) persons who directly observed an event relevant to the violation; (d) persons identified by the complainant or the alleged violator who may possess relevant information; (e) administrators, managers, coaches, or supervisors of the complainant and the alleged violator; (f) persons whom the complainant and the alleged violator requested that the institution interview; and (g) persons identified in documents or other information who may possess relevant information (Poteet 2001, 15).

The interview process should not turn into a fishing expedition in which anybody and everybody are interviewed by the investigator (Poteet 2001, 15). In fact, the internal investigator should limit "the number of interviews to only those reasonably determined to have relevant information" (Poteet 2001, 15). However, even if an interview is well-planned, a follow-up interview or interviews may be needed in some instances (Potuto 2004, 5; Poteet 2001, 15).

Interview Preparation

Preparation is essential to conducting an effective and useful investigative interview. The internal investigator should review the investigative chart, prior interview notes, and relevant documents before conducting an interview. These exercises will provide the investigator with a better understanding of the case. Furthermore, the document review and investigative chart will identify questions and issues that should be explored during the interview. Finally, the investigator should prepare an outline of the interview questions in advance.

As an investigator prepares for an interview, he or she should anticipate addressing four categories of issues before or during the interview.

First, internal investigators should consider the timetable in interviewing employees, student-athletes, and other persons since an interview subject's recollection of past events may often favor the party who conducts the first examination (Buckner 2002; Marshall 1999).

Second, the internal investigator should be prepared to explain to the interview subject the relationship between the internal investigator and the institution, including the fact that the investigator does not represent the employee, student-athlete, or athletic representative (Marshall 1999; Kuehne 1997, 680). This type of communication will reduce confusion as to whose interests the internal investigator represents (Marshall 1999; Kuehne 1997, 680).

Third, the investigator should be prepared to discuss the role of the NCAA enforcement staff in the process, including the fact that NCAA investigators may contact interview subjects directly and seek to interview them (Marshall 1999). Also, if the interview subject is an institutional employee, a student, or an athletic representative, the investigator should be prepared to explain the interview subject's obligations to respond to inquiries by the institution and the NCAA under NCAA Bylaws 19 and 32.

Finally, effective interviews occur when an investigator keeps in mind the following: (a) if possible, conduct the interview at locations that can protect the privacy of the interview subject and the confidentiality of the information; (b) conduct the interview in a professional manner; (c) keep the interview focused on issues pertinent to the investigation and avoid turning the discussion into a gripe session on irrelevant grievances; (d) keep accurate and detailed notes; and (e) consider what documents, if any, the interview subject should be questioned on and bring copies of identified documents to the interview (Buckner 2002; Poteet 2001, 16–19).

Notification of the Interview Purpose and the Interview Subject's Rights

Before starting an interview, the internal investigator should provide the interview subject with a written and/or oral statement disclosing the purpose of the interview. The language of the statement should be based, in part, on the content of NCAA legislation, which provides that when an enforcement investigator requests information that could be detrimental to an individual's interests, that individual shall be advised that the purpose of the interview is to determine whether he or she has been involved directly or indirectly in any violation of NCAA legislation. Prior to an interview arranged or initiated by the enforcement staff, a student-athlete or staff member must be advised that if the individual has violated the NCAA's ethical conduct legislation such an allegation may be forthcoming based upon the individual's:

- Involvement in violations.
- Refusal to furnish information relevant to the investigation of a possible violation when requested by the NCAA or by the institution.
- Provision of false or misleading information to the NCAA, conference, or institution concerning the individual's knowledge of or involvement in a violation.

The statement should also inform the interview subject that: (a) cooperation is a necessity; (b) the institution has retained the internal investigator to represent the institution in connection with its investigation; (c) the interview is voluntary and the subject may request that it be terminated at any time, but under NCAA legislation institutional employees, student-athletes, or athletic representatives may face consequences for terminating an interview; (d) the institution recommends that the subject consult with counsel before any interview, but it is the subject's decision whether to do so; (e) the subject must be truthful when providing answers to questions during the interview; and (f) information provided during the interview will be kept confidential (Buckner 2002; Marshall 1999). However, when an internal investigator advises an interview subject of his or her rights, the investigator should not suggest that the subject refuse to speak with the NCAA enforcement staff., which would be a violation of NCAA enforcement legislation (Buckner 2002; Marshall 1999; Kuehne 1997, 680).

If the institution has a policy of providing an attorney to personnel, the investigator should also advise the interview subject about the following: (a) the option to consult with counsel independent of the institution's lawyers; (b) the role of separate counsel (i.e., to advise the interview subject as to the nature of the internal investigation, the purpose of the interview, and the subject's rights and obligations in connection with the interview); and (c) the institution's agreement to cover the fees and related expenses for the subject's legal representation in connection with the internal investigation (Marshall 1999).

Interview Techniques

An internal investigator's application of basic interview techniques can increase the success of any interview. An investigator should use the following techniques during an interview (Buckner 2002; Poteet 2001, 19–20):

- Permit the subject to offer answers in a free and comfortable environment.
- If necessary, restate information on important issues or points to confirm that the investigator and the interview subject are in agreement about what was discussed.
- If necessary, simplify a series of questions or statements to encourage more complete responses to questions.
- Eliminate telegraphing the "right" answer to a question by refraining from an interviewer's natural tendency to talk a great deal.
- Avoid interrupting the subject, which can risk cutting off the conclusion of the subject's response.
- Remain silent after the subject completes an answer. This technique can cause a subject to continue talking in order to fill in the silence.
- Use introduction questions (e.g., what is your name, where did you attend college, where do you live) to obtain an interview subject's "baseline" body language (e.g., posture, arm position, eye contact). Observe any deviations from the baseline when the interview proceeds into difficult questioning. A deviation may indicate: (a) the subject is uncomfortable with the question or response; or (b) the subject is providing false or misleading information.
- Use the "funnel technique," which involves starting with broad and open-ended questions on a topic or an issue and ending the discussion with narrow and detailed questions.

- Ask any unfriendly or embarrassing questions at the end of the interview since these questions may cause a subject to become defensive if posed at the beginning of the interview.
- Maintain a list of documents provided to each subject during an interview.
- Ask questions that will produce relevant facts, suitable leads, or potential interview subjects.
- Use "who, what, when, where, how, and why" questions on every topic and issue.
- Refrain from offering any opinions or conclusions.
- If needed, follow up an interview subject's response with additional questions or issues that may not be on the prepared interview outline.
- Close out a series of questions on a topic or an issue by posing a closing question, including "Anything else?"
- Confirm that the subject's recollection has been exhausted on all pertinent issues and topics by asking appropriate follow-up questions and checking interview notes to see if all areas have been covered thoroughly.
- At the conclusion of the interview, ask the subject if there were any questions that could have been asked but were not. The response may identify topics or issues unknown to the investigator.

Recording the Interview

Contrary to the common internal investigative practice in some industries, most (if not all) interviews conducted in the NCAA enforcement process are recorded through the use of a mechanical device. NCAA legislation requires the enforcement staff to record interviews whenever possible. The bylaws also permit an institution to record interviews in which an institutional representative is present or to do so jointly with the NCAA enforcement staff. To guarantee that the committee will consider all of the institution's evidence obtained from an interview, an internal investigator should follow the enforcement staff's practice and tape-record investigative interviews, if practical.

If a subject objects to the recording of the interview, an investigator can prepare a written statement of the interview. An investigator also can prepare a written statement in situations when: (a) an interview cannot be tape-recorded; or (b) the recording device malfunctions. An investigator should obtain a confirmation of the statement's accuracy with the subject's dated signature. The investigator should permit the subject to make additions or corrections to the statement before the signed confirmation is obtained. However, NCAA legislation gives the committee on infractions the authority to consider testimony as to the substance of an unrecorded interview for which a signed affirmation was not obtained to the extent the committee determines the testimony to be reliable.

Generally, the NCAA enforcement staff will not disclose to an institution and involved individual a written statement prepared by the staff during an investigation. However, the enforcement staff's written statements become available to the institution and involved individuals when the staff provides access to its investigative file at the custodial site.

Investigators should be aware of a few additional issues concerning recording interviews. First, NCAA legislation permits the subject to record the interview. Second, institutions can provide the subject with a copy of the recording only if the subject signs a statement of confidentiality. Third, a statement of confidentiality consists of the subject's agreement not to release tape-recordings or interview transcripts to a third party. The investigator should have the subject sign or, if necessary, orally record a statement of confidentiality prior to an interview. Fourth, during interviews conducted by the enforcement staff, investigators are permitted to take handwritten notes of an interview.

Employees and Internal Investigations

Legal Representation of Employees in an Investigation

Under NCAA legislation, an institution is responsible for the actions of its administrators, students, employees, and athletic representatives. Thus the conduct of persons at the institution will be the focus of an internal investigation and the NCAA enforcement staff's inquiry. Because of these issues, an internal investigator should consider as soon as possible whether separate legal counsel should represent these individuals (Marshall 1999).

In fact, administrators and coaches who are targets of an institution's internal investigation or an NCAA inquiry may require separate counsel on an individual basis (Marshall 1999). As a result, when an institution is the subject or the target of an NCAA investigation, a potential conflict of interest arises between it and its employees (Marshall 1999).

If the institution determines that an employee will be a source of information rather than a target of its investigation or the NCAA inquiry, then joint representation by institutional counsel may be appropriate (Marshall 1999). However, an employee's status as a witness, subject, or target of an NCAA investigation may change as the internal investigation progresses (Marshall 1999). This may present future challenges if joint representation is undertaken at the beginning of an internal investigation and a conflict emerges between the institution and the employee (Marshall 1999).

The institution also must determine early in the internal investigation whether it will provide counsel to its employees at institutional expense. Under the laws of many states, institutions may be required to indemnify (i.e., to protect against damage, loss, or injury) an employee even in the context of an NCAA inquiry (Marshall 1999). However, the institution should analyze whether the employee's conduct was within his or her duties (Marshall 1999). Most important, an institution may not be required to protect an employee against damage, loss, or injury if his or her conduct was inconsistent with the documented duties for the employee's position (Marshall 1999).

Finally, the institution should avoid the risk of angering personnel and having them become an adverse party in the enforcement process. A disgruntled employee also can file a lawsuit against the institution during the internal investigation (Marshall 1999). Both scenarios create additional challenges that can be avoided through adequate planning and strategic use of employment actions.

Preparing Employees for Interviews Conducted by the NCAA Enforcement Staff

An institution can decide whether to conduct a preparation session for personnel who will be interviewed by the NCAA enforcement staff or athletic conference officials. However, a session should not be a complicated production. Moreover, a preparation session should not be used to coach an interview subject but to facilitate the enforcement and conference staffs' ability to obtain accurate information during the interview. Specifically, the interview subject should be instructed to: (a) provide honest testimony; (b) listen carefully to each question posed by the NCAA or conference investigator and provide a complete answer; (c) clarify whether the answer is based on information that the person "knew or understood at the time of the events at issue" or from what the interview subject learned subsequent to that time; (d) refrain from providing answers based on conjecture or speculation (Marshall 1999).

Likewise, if an internal investigator reviews documents with an interview subject, the investigator must be careful to avoid a "selective presentation" that could lead the NCAA enforcement staff and athletic conference officials to believe that the institution attempted to mislead the subject and improperly influence the testimony (Marshall 1999). Finally, internal investigators should not coach a person so that his or her factual knowledge or understanding becomes consistent with other parties' testimony (Buckner 2002; Marshall 1999).

CHAPTER 4

PROACTIVE STRATEGIES
FOR ADMINISTRATORS,
COACHES, AND EMPLOYEES
WHO ARE TARGETS OF
AN INVESTIGATION

It is probable that an athletic administrator, coach, or other institutional official may be named, in his or her individual capacity, as a violator of NCAA legislation at some point during an institution's or NCAA enforcement staff's inquiry. This section outlines the measures athletic administrators and coaches can use if they become a target of an investigation.

Retention of Legal Counsel or Private Investigators

If an athletic administrator, coach, or other institutional official is alleged to have committed a major violation of NCAA legislation, it is wise for the alleged party to retain an attorney or a private investigator experienced in the NCAA enforcement process. The involvement of an attorney or private investigator at an early stage in the process permits the administrator or coach to defend allegations more effectively (Morrison 1999, 2). The retention of outside expertise also will limit an investigation's interference in an administrator's or a coach's job duties (Morrison 1999, 2). Finally, NCAA Bylaws 19 and 32 provide administrators and coaches the right to have legal counsel during investigation interviews (Morrison 1999, 2).

An administrator or a coach should follow a six-step process when choosing an attorney or private investigator (Florida Bar 2003; AAFC 2004).

First, an administrator or a coach should identify prospective attorneys and private investigators by asking colleagues and industry associations for referrals or by searching electronic databases and directories, including Martindale-Hubble (Florida Bar 2003; AAFC 2004). In addition, some institutions may provide and pay for an attorney or investigative services for an administrator or coach during an investigation.

Second, an administrator or a coach should prepare a list of the desired characteristics in an attorney or private investigator (Florida Bar 2003).

Third, an administrator or a coach should request basic information from each law or investigation firm. In particular, an administrator or a coach should ask about experience, costs, fees and fee structures (e.g., invoice schedule, installment plan), services, and references (Florida Bar 2003; AAFC 2004). The administrator or a coach should review the information provided, check references, and narrow the candidate field to three or four parties. An in-person meeting or conference call should be scheduled with each of the finalists.

Fourth, an administrator or a coach should determine personal chemistry with the prospective attorney or private investigator. In particular, during the in-person meeting or conference call, an administrator or a coach should focus on factors concerning chemistry and trust (Florida Bar 2003). This is important because an administrator or a coach should not hire an attorney or a private investigator if he or she seems dishonest or does not provide a comfortable working relationship (Florida Bar 2003). In addition, an administrator or a coach should request responses to the following questions (Florida Bar 2003):

- What kind of outcome does the attorney or private investigator expect?
- How often will he or she be in contact?
- How quickly are phone calls returned?
- If the attorney or private investigator is not in the office, can someone else handle emergencies and urgent questions?
- How experienced is the attorney or private investigator? Ask how many NCAA enforcement cases he or she has handled.

Fifth, an administrator or a coach should use the information obtained from the in-person meeting or conference call, as well as the previously submitted documentation, to select an appropriate representative (AAFC 2004). An administrator or a coach should inform all candidates of the decision.

Sixth, an administrator or a coach should keep copies of any engagement or retainer agreements and invoices (Florida Bar 2003). An administrator or a coach should request an engagement or retainer agreement if one is not provided (Florida Bar 2003). An *engagement* or *retainer agreement* is the contract that states what services the legal counsel or private investigator will provide as well as the fees and costs for such services (AAFC 2004; Florida Bar 2003). Some states require attorneys to provide a written statement of clients' rights. Finally, administrators and coaches should request a receipt for any payments made for legal or consulting services (Florida Bar 2003).

Defensive and Offensive Plans for Athletic Administrators and Coaches

Administrators and coaches targeted during an investigation or named in an institutional report or NCAA notice of allegations should take the following steps (Morrison 1999, 2–4):

- Review the allegations. Review the institution's investigative reports and the NCAA notices of inquiry and allegations. The documents will describe the scope, nature, pertinent facts, documents, and parties involved in the case.
- Be professional. Administrators and coaches should not panic and should conduct themselves professionally when dealing with institutional and NCAA and conference investigators.
- Conduct an independent inquiry. An administrator or coach, with the assistance of an attorney or a private investigator, should conduct an inquiry to collect any relevant facts, witnesses, documents, or other information. Investigations by the institution and the NCAA may not have uncovered all the pertinent information in the case. This will be helpful when an administrator or a coach prepares a response to a notice of allegations or develops a presentation for the committee on infractions hearing.
- Respond to document requests. The institution and the NCAA will request documents and electronic records pertaining to the case. Administrators and coaches should ask for the request to be made in writing. (A copy of the request should be maintained by the administrator or coach.) The written request should also contain: (a) the specific scope of the request; (b) the specific documents or categories of documents requested; (c) the date by which the documents must be produced; and (d) what organization (e.g., institution, conference, NCAA) should receive the documents. The administrator or coach should keep his or her attorney or private investigator apprised of any request for documents. If investigators drop by an administrator's or a coach's office to search for documents, a request should be made for a representative to be present during the search.

- Keep copies of documents. Administrators and coaches should keep copies of all documents produced to investigators whenever possible. If computers or software are seized, an administrator or a coach should request a backup copy of the relevant programs or data files. In addition, an accurate list of documents produced to the institution and enforcement staff should be maintained so that the administrator's or coach's attorney or private investigator can request copies or the return of the documents at the earliest possible time.
- Maintain evidence. Administrators and coaches must never alter, conceal, or destroy information relevant to an investigation.
- Be cooperative. Administrators and coaches should cooperate with investigators but should confer with an attorney or private investigator(s) throughout the NCAA enforcement process to protect their legal rights.

CHAPTER 5

SELF-REPORTS, SELF-DISCLOSURES, AND COMMUNICATIONS TO THE NCAA ENFORCEMENT STAFF

Reports for Internal Purposes

Internal investigators should prepare a memorandum or report to the institution after the completion of the internal investigation. The memorandum or report should contain the following information (Buckner 2002; Marshall 1999; Kuehne 1997, 681):

- A summary of facts uncovered during the internal investigation.
- An analysis of NCAA legislation concerning the facts of the case.
- An analysis of any weaknesses in the institution's practices or procedures.
- A discussion of any arguments against the imposition of NCAA or athletic conference sanctions.
- A list of recommendations for corrective actions, self-imposed penalties, and other measures that would improve institutional practices and enhance the institution's position in the case.

The memorandum or report assists internal investigators in developing a strategy concerning the case. The report also provides a basis for the development of the institution's written submissions to the NCAA enforcement staff, athletic conference officials, and the committee on infractions. However, if the institution believes that the NCAA will issue a notice of allegation, a detailed report of the internal investigation's findings can cause problems (Marshall 1999; Kuehne 1997, 681). For instance, an unauthorized disclosure of the report can adversely affect the institution's position in the enforcement process as well as severely harm its public relations posture (Marshall 1999; Kuehne 1997, 681). If this is a major concern, internal investigators should consider providing the institution with an oral report (Marshall 1999).

The memorandum or report should be marked "confidential" or "privileged" if it can be classified as a communication protected by the attorney-client privilege and/or work-product doctrine (Marshall 1999; Kuehne 1997, 681). Furthermore, the privileged status of the memorandum or report can be preserved if it is presented only to the institution's board of regents/trustees, special investigation committee, or senior administrators (Marshall 1999; Kuehne 1997, 681). Copies of the internal investigation report should be collected and stored in a secure area (Marshall 1999; Kuehne 1997, 681).

Self-Reports and Self-Disclosures to the NCAA

An institution can submit two types of reports to the NCAA enforcement staff and athletic conference officials. A *self-report* is the document provided by an institution to the NCAA enforcement staff that reports secondary or major violations of NCAA legislation that have already been reported to the institution's athletic conference or the NCAA (Enforcement 2001, 1).

A *self-disclosure* is a type of self-report submitted to the NCAA when the institution uncovers a violation before it was reported to the institution's athletic conference or to the NCAA. The committee on infractions can consider the self-disclosure of information during its review of possible corrective and punitive actions. The committee also may consider the efforts of the institution to assist in the development of complete information. The committee generally provides more credit if the institution self-discloses (Enforcement 2001, 1–2). In addition, the committee examines the institution's efforts to review information concerning possible violations (Enforcement 2001, 1–2). Conversely, the committee has found member institutions in violation of NCAA Constitution 2.1.1 and 2.8.1 and Bylaw 14.1.2 if they have not adequately reviewed information concerning possible violations or have not reported violations (Enforcement 2001, 1–2).

An institution's obligation to self-report or self-disclose possible violations of NCAA legislation (Enforcement 2001, 1–2) is provided in:

- NCAA Constitution 2.8.1, which explains an institution's responsibility to identify and report to the NCAA "instances in which compliance has not been achieved" and to take appropriate corrective actions.
- NCAA Constitution 3.2.4.3, which requires an institution to certify the eligibility of student-athletes in accordance with NCAA legislation and to apply immediately all applicable rules, including withholding all ineligible student-athletes from competition.
- NCAA Constitution 3.2.4.3, which provides that if a violation is alleged to have occurred involving a student-athlete with eligibility

remaining, the institution has the responsibility to review the information to determine whether the student-athlete's eligibility is affected.

- NCAA Bylaw 14.01.1, which prohibits an institution from using a student-athlete in competition unless the student-athlete meets all applicable eligibility requirements.

However, an institution is not required to report to the enforcement staff if it is unable to determine whether a violation occurred or concludes that no violations occurred (Enforcement 2001, 1–2). In such instance, the institution is encouraged to advise the enforcement staff of its conclusion and to keep a written record of the methodology used and the results of the inquiry (Enforcement 2001, 2).

Presenting an Argument Not to Issue a Notice of Allegations

An internal investigation can uncover undisputed information that does not support the issuance of a notice of allegations by the NCAA enforcement staff. The institution's findings can also support a reduction of the scope of the notice of allegations. If the evidence supports either position, the institution should make an in-person presentation to the NCAA enforcement staff (Marshall 1999). If the institution elects to make a presentation, it is advisable to obtain the NCAA enforcement staff's advance agreement that the presentation is made without prejudice to the institution and (if pertinent) without waiver of the attorney-client privilege and work-product doctrine (Marshall 1999).

According to legal commentator Raymond C. Marshall (1999), an institution can use several arguments to support the nonissuance of a notice of allegations or the limited scope of the notice:

- The facts do not support an inference of knowledge or intent of wrongdoing.
- The committee on infractions would not issue major sanctions if the case were brought to a hearing.
- Prosecution would serve no NCAA regulatory interest.
- The conduct in question is a law enforcement priority relative to other areas.

- Prosecution is unnecessary to achieve deterrence.
- There is no evidence of fraudulent motivation.
- The institution has no history of violations and an excellent record of public service.
- The institution made timely disclosure and has been and will continue to be fully cooperative with the investigation conducted by the NCAA enforcement staff.
- The adverse consequences of prosecution, including disruption of important campus/athletic programs and economic dislocation of an institution's workforce, would be contrary to the public interest. (This argument is often not persuasive, because almost any institution can make it,)
- The misconduct is geographically and organizationally isolated.
- The institution has in place effective systems for preventing, detecting, and correcting improper activity.
- The institution took or will take strong disciplinary action against the person or persons who committed the violation.

Even when these factors do not prevent the issuance of a notice of allegations, Marshall suggests they may be useful to help persuade the NCAA enforcement staff to:

- Reduce the number of violations charged.
- Limit the scope of the possible sanctions.
- Charge a secondary violation instead of a major violation.
- Charge no individuals.
- Intercede on the institution's behalf with the committee on infractions.

PART 3

BEST PRACTICES, REPORT FORMATS AND CITATIONS, AND INVESTIGATION RESOURCES

CHAPTER 1

ATHLETIC INVESTIGATION
BEST PRACTICES

This chapter provides an overview of best practices that can be used by institutions and involved individuals to address critical issues associated with internal investigations and the NCAA enforcement process.

Document Investigation Policy and Procedure

An institution should have a documented policy and procedure for conducting internal investigations (Potuto 2004, 4; Enforcement 2001, 3). NCAA Constitution 2.1.1 and 2.8.1 and Bylaw 14.1.2 provide the committees on infractions with the authority to review whether an institution has an investigation policy (Enforcement 2001, 3). The committees also are responsible for determining whether the policy was followed during an investigation (Enforcement 2001, 3). A comprehensive investigation policy and procedure should address: (a) what specific event triggers an inquiry; (b) how complaints, tips, rumors, and anonymous reports concerning possible violations of NCAA legislation are received and reviewed; and (c) who conducts the inquiry (Potuto 2004, 1; Enforcement 2001, 3). Finally, the institution's investigation policy and procedure should include a methodology to review possible secondary violations (Enforcement 2001, 3). Overall, an investigation policy and procedure should include the following elements (Potuto 2004, 1, 6; Marsh and Robbins 2003, 697; Enforcement 2001, 3–4):

- Expectation statement documenting the obligation of institutional personnel, students, and athletic representatives to report possible violations of NCAA legislation.
- Procedures designed to impose "immediate and severe consequences" for failing to report alleged violations of NCAA legislation or to act immediately once an alleged violation is discovered.
- Regularly scheduled compliance meetings with the compliance officer, compliance staff, faculty athletics representative, initial-eligibility certifying officer, and other personnel with compliance-related duties. The meetings enable personnel with compliance-related duties to share or piece together rumors or possible allegations of improper conduct.

- Procedures designating an institutional official as responsible for contacting the NCAA vice president for enforcement services when the institution has determined it will investigate allegations of possible major violations.
- Procedures governing how internal investigators will be retained or appointed.
- Procedures to conduct an independent and thorough investigation and plan the investigation report. The procedures also should require the report's submission to the institutional administrators, including the chief executive officer and the director of athletics, within a reasonable period.
- Procedures defining clear responsibilities for administrators (including the director of athletics, compliance coordinator, faculty athletics representative, and general counsel) during an investigation.
- Procedures to address and correct identified deficiencies in policies, procedures, and processes within the institution and the athletics program.
- Procedures for reporting violations, corrective measures, and self-imposed penalties to the institution's athletic conference and to the NCAA enforcement staff.
- Procedures to incorporate the investigation policy and procedure into the athletic compliance education program.

Contact the NCAA Enforcement Staff about Alleged Violations

The NCAA enforcement staff advises a member institution to contact the staff when the institution decides to conduct an investigation of alleged major violations (Enforcement 2001, 3–4). The institution can notify the staff by telephone (Enforcement 2001, 4). However, the NCAA advises institutions to prepare a written record of the communication (Enforcement 2001, 4). If the allegations are known to the general public, the institution's communication allows the staff to know that the institution is addressing the issues through a prompt inquiry (Enforcement 2001, 4). If the information is not public, the communication is seen as an application of the cooperative principle (Enforcement 2001, 4). In addition, if the staff understands that an institution is conducting an inquiry regarding information the enforcement staff also possesses, it may be a factor in the extent, if any, of the staff's inquiries (Enforcement 2001, 4).

Prepare for, Follow Up, and Document Investigative Interviews and Physical Evidence

An institution's or involved individual's investigator can perform a thorough and effective inquiry if the following items are addressed (Potuto 2004, 4–6; Buckner 2002):

- If practical, collect as many documents, computer files, phone records, and any other relevant materials as possible before conducting interviews.
- Include two institutional investigators at all interviews or, at a minimum, at significant interviews.
- At a minimum, tape-record all interviews that will be relied on in preparing a self-report, a response to the notice of allegations, or a hearing presentation. If questions of privilege are not at issue, all interviews should be tape-recorded.
- Interview individuals separately.
- Investigators can use one of two strategies to schedule interviews: (a) interview persons most critical to the inquiry before knowledge of the investigation, or their direct involvement in the alleged violations, reaches the press or public, prohibiting the interview subject from crafting a "story"; or (b) interview targeted persons at the end of the inquiry, arming an internal investigator with the full weight of knowledge from the entire investigation. Each strategy has its disadvantages and advantages.
- Follow up on any relevant sources, including interviews and collected evidence.
- Maintain the chain of custody for evidence collected during the investigation.

Do Not Treat a Committee on Infractions Hearing Like a Criminal or Civil Trial

Lawyers for institutions and involved individuals should not apply civil and criminal litigation tactics in the NCAA enforcement process, especially during a committee on infractions hearing. In fact, emotional arguments and pleas used in a criminal or civil trial often are not effective in a committee on infractions hearing and can erode the effectiveness of the hearing presentation (Marsh and Robbins 2003, 679).

Embrace the Cooperative Principle

An investigation by an institution or involved individual should be consistent with the cooperative principle. The principle imposes an affirmative obligation on an NCAA member institution and institutional personnel and athletic representatives to assist the NCAA enforcement staff in developing full information to determine whether a possible violation of NCAA legislation has occurred and the details of the violation.

Prepare a Public Relations/Crisis Management Policy and Plan Before a Scandal Hits

A comprehensive public relations and crisis management plan should be prepared by the institution prior to any scandal. The policy and plan should (Marsh and Robbins 2003, 676–77; Buckner 2002):

- Designate the institutional contact person for the press and public.
- Describe what information will be addressed to the press and the public.
- Provide guidance for the chief executive officer, athletic administrators, faculty, coaches, and student-athletes in dealing with the press and the public during an enforcement case.
- Coordinate the duties of the university relations officer, spokesperson, and sports information director.

Provide Detailed Information in Reports
to the NCAA Enforcement Staff

According to the NCAA enforcement staff, the following are common errors that may occur during the internal investigation or in the preparation of a report to the NCAA (Enforcement 2001, 4–6):

- Failure to follow the institution's investigation policy and plan.
- Failure to notify, orally or in writing prior to an interview, student-athletes and institutional personnel of the ethical obligations under NCAA legislation (NCAA Bylaw 10.1).
- Failure to recognize student-athlete eligibility issues. An institution is obligated to conduct an immediate assessment of information about a student-athlete who is practicing and/or representing the institution in competition. An institution's eligibility determination should be: (a) based on available information; and (b) documented (including the reasons for the institution's position). The institution also should understand that its eligibility assessment may change if additional information is collected as the investigation proceeds.
- Failure to submit the necessary information in a self-report or self-disclosure.
- Failure to state the specific violation the institution is reporting to the staff.
- Failure to incorporate and categorize all documentation and other information relevant to the case, including all records that "corroborate or refute the information reported by all involved parties."
- Failure to implement meaningful corrective or punitive actions. The NCAA enforcement staff advises that "the institution should review the nature of the violations and determine the impact of the proposed penalties" while "determining corrective and punitive actions." Institutions should "consider implementing punitive actions in the general area in which the violations occurred" when assessing the nature of the violations.

CHAPTER 2

FORMATTING AN INSTITUTIONAL SELF-REPORT

Formatting an Institutional Self-Report or Self-Disclosure

Once an internal investigation concludes, an institution is required to submit its findings to the NCAA enforcement staff and athletic conference officials. A well-prepared and organized report assists an institution in communicating its investigation to the NCAA enforcement staff and athletic conference officials. At a minimum, an institutional self-report or self-disclosure should address the following topics (Enforcement 2001, 10–15):

- An introduction.
- The purpose of the report.
- A case chronology.
- A general overview of findings.
- The nature of violations.
- The identities and titles of all involved individuals named in an allegation (including biographical background for each party).
- An overview of the institution's investigation.
- The date and the means by which the institution became aware of the information.
- The methodology used during the investigation.
- The length of the institution's investigation.
- The number of individuals interviewed by the institution and their relationship to the inquiry.
- The means used by the institution to locate individuals interviewed.
- The identities of individuals who refused to be interviewed or who were not located.
- Specific findings and narrative.
- A statement of finding.
- Mitigating and aggravating factors.
- Supportive narrative for each finding.
- Other possible violations.
- Corrective actions and penalties.
- Corrective actions implemented or proposed by the institution.
- Penalties self-imposed or proposed by the institution.

- Background information on the institution and involved individuals.
- Background information for each involved sport, including grant-in-aid information, regular-season records, postseason records, average number of official paid visits during the previous four academic years, a current squad list form, and other relevant information. Documentation should be included in an appendix to the report.
- A conclusion.
- An appendix.

Example of a "Specific Findings and Narrative Section" in an Institutional Report

The following provides an example of a "Specific Findings and Narrative Section" in an institutional report. A findings section also can include other elements, including, but not limited to: summary of the allegation; the cause of the violation; violation level; and mitigating factors. The level of detail will depend on the nature of the violation and the complexity of the facts at issue.

I. **Provision of Extra Benefits to a Men's Volleyball Student-Athlete by a Representative of the Institution's Athletics Interests. [NCAA Bylaws 16.02.3, 16.12.2.1, and 16.12.2.3 (2003-04 NCAA Division I Manual)]**

A. Finding

On October 30, 2003, John Lotsofmoney, a representative of the institution's athletics interests, provided six hundred dollars in cash to then-men's volleyball student-athlete Ron Blocker in the student-athlete's apartment. Lotsofmoney provided the cash to Blocker so that the student-athlete could host an off-campus Halloween party on October 31, 2003. Blocker used approximately four hundred dollars to purchase supplies for the nonalcoholic party and deposited the remaining funds into his checking account for future personal use.

B. Supporting Narrative

1. Discovery of the Violation

The violation described in the above finding was discovered during the May 1, 2004, exit interview of then-men's volleyball student-athlete Ron Blocker.

2. Overview of Reported Information and Reasons for Violation

During the May 1, 2004, exit interview of then-men's volleyball student-athlete Ron Blocker, assistant athletics director for compliance Gail Resourceful learned that John Lotsofmoney, a representative of the institution's athletics interests, provided six hundred dollars in cash to men's volleyball student-athlete Ron Blocker. Specifically, Blocker informed Resourceful that at approximately 2 p.m. on October 30, 2003, Lotsofmoney provided him with six hundred dollars in cash during a visit by the representative to the student-athlete's apartment. Audiotape recording of 5/1/04 interview of Ron Blocker. Blocker explained that Lotsofmoney occasionally dropped by his apartment to chat about academics and athletics. Audiotape recording of 5/1/04 interview of Ron Blocker. Blocker recalled that during the October 30 visit, he mentioned to Lotsofmoney the Halloween party he was hosting the next day. Audiotape recording of 5/1/04 interview of Ron Blocker. The party, which Blocker described as a nonalcoholic event, was to be held in Blocker's off-campus apartment. Audiotape recording of 5/1/04 interview of Ron Blocker. Lotsofmoney offered to underwrite the party and provided six hundred dollars in cash to Blocker for that purpose. Audiotape recording of 5/1/04 interview of Ron Blocker. Later that afternoon, Blocker used approximately four hundred dollars to purchase supplies for the party from the Student Discount Market, a local supermarket. Audiotape recording of 5/1/04 interview of Ron Blocker; App. 3. Blocker informed Resourceful that he deposited the remaining funds into his checking account for future personal use. Audiotape recording of 5/1/04 interview of Ron Blocker. Lotsofmoney declined to be interviewed by the institution on several occasions. App. 5.

Blocker informed the institution that this was the first and only time that Lotsofmoney had offered or provided him with cash or any other extra benefits. Audiotape recording of 5/1/04 interview of Ron Blocker. Blocker is not aware of Lotsofmoney offering or providing extra benefits to student-athletes or improper inducements to prospective student-athletes. Audiotape recording of 5/1/04 interview of Ron Blocker. Based on Blocker's cooperation and written permission, the institution's subsequent investigation obtained copies of receipts for the party supplies and the student-athlete's checking account records. App. 3. The records verify Blocker's testimony.

The institution's investigation revealed that the violation occurred because of the intentional actions of Lotsofmoney and Blocker to disregard NCAA legislation. Audiotape recording of 5/1/04 interview of Ron Blocker. In fact, despite the conduct of monthly rules education sessions and the submission of compliance-related materials to Blocker and Lotsofmoney (through his membership in a booster organization), Blocker admitted that they were aware of the applicable legislation and decided to disregard such provisions when the cash exchange took place on October 30. Audiotape recording of 5/1/04 interview of Ron Blocker; App. 6.

3. Student-Athlete Eligibility Issues

The institution determined that the eligibility of Blocker is not implicated because the student-athlete has graduated from the institution and has exhausted his eligibility. App. 2.

CHAPTER 3

CITATION AND REFERENCE SUGGESTIONS FOR INFRACTIONS REPORTS

A report (including self-reports, responses to notice of allegations and appellate briefs) to the NCAA committee on infractions, infractions appeals committee, and enforcement staff is based on investigative materials collected during an internal investigation or a review of the enforcement staff's investigation file. A well-written report uses a logical and consistent system to reference evidence in the record. The purpose of a citation and reference system is to help committee members, enforcement staff, athletic conference officials, and other readers locate investigation sources accurately and efficiently. This chapter provides guidance for citing and referencing NCAA case precedent and legislation, investigative materials, and other resources directly in the body of a report. If supporting materials are submitted in an appendix, however, the citation of the materials should correspond with their location in the appendix.

General Formatting Suggestions

The enforcement staff includes a "Suggested Guidelines for Submission of Responses" or similar document with a notice of allegations. The document, prepared by the committee on infractions, contains several suggested formatting guidelines for preparing and submitting responses to the notice of allegations. For example, the committee says a response to the notice of allegations should be "contained in either three-ring loose-leaf or 'comb' style binders"; however, the committee prefers comb-style binder). Further, according to the committee, a response to a notice allegations should be "separated by numbered tabs corresponding to the allegation numbers in the notice of allegations so as to be easily referenced by the reader." In addition, a response "should be paginated," and the committee suggests "that each allegation have its own set of page numbers." The committee provides the following example: "page one of the section on allegation 1 would be page 1–1, page 6 of the section on Allegation No. 4 would be page 4–6, etc." Finally, the committee says "each allegation response should contain the allegation itself, the position of the responding party to the allegation (agree or disagree) and the rationale/supporting evidence for the position."

Appendix

A report may include an appendix containing the investigative materials and other relevant information the NCAA committee on infractions, infractions appeals committee, or enforcement need during the review of a case.

Appendix in a Report to the Enforcement Staff and Appellate Briefs

An appendix to a report to the enforcement staff or a brief to the infractions appeals committee should include a copy of pertinent materials from the case record (including, but not limited to, physical evidence, articles, letters, exhibits, interview transcripts, memoranda, case precedent, or interpretations). Appendix numbers (e.g., App. A, App. 1) can be placed in a consistent place (e.g., the bottom of document or tabs) or preceding each item. The items also should be listed in a table of contents at the front of the appendix. The appendix can be separately bound or, if it is not voluminous, included at the end of a report. The appendix contents should be clearly referenced in the report. The basic form is:

Appendix or App. number (including internal document number or paragraph, if necessary)

An example of this form:

Specifically, from December 17, 2002, to June 1, 2004, the director of athletics was the sole signatory on a local bank account in the name of "State University Athletics." App. 1; App. 2 at p. 12. The account was maintained as a private account and was not disclosed to anyone outside the athletics department. App. 2 at p. 12. From January 2003 through June 2004, the director of athletics misappropriated $201,345 of university money by depositing it in the private account. App. 2 at pp. 12–13; App. 3. Approximately $175,669 of this amount was derived from at least seventy-five checks made payable to the university and sent to the director of athletics for appropriate disposition. App. 2 at pp. 13–14; App. 3. The former associate athletic director verified this information. App. 4 and 5.

Michael L. Buckner

Appendix to a Response to a Notice of Allegations

An appendix to a response to a notice of allegations should be formatted using the document "Suggested Guidelines for Submission of Responses" (or other committee-supplied resource) as a reference. The document, which is included by the enforcement staff with a notice of allegations, is prepared by the committee on infractions to provide parties with several suggested formatting guidelines for preparing and submitting responses to the notice of allegations.

Identification of Persons

Persons in Current Positions

When first identifying a person in a report to the NCAA enforcement staff, athletic conference officials, the committees on infractions, and the infractions appeals committees, indicate the person and the person's title and organization. The full title and first name of the person can be omitted on subsequent references to the person in the report. The basic forms are:

Organization, title or position, name of person
or
Name of person, organization, title or position

Examples of this form include:

On February 1, 2004, State University director of athletics Mary Administrator was interviewed for the purposes of the institution's internal investigation. During the interview, the director of athletics testified ...
or
The institution admits that John Lotsofmoney, a representative of the institution's athletics interests, provided numerous extra benefits to student-athletes. Specifically, Lotsofmoney extended an interest-free loan ...

Persons Formerly in Positions

However, if a person held a title at some point prior to the submission of the report, the word *then* should be inserted before the title. The basic forms are:

Then (organization, title or position, name of person)
or
(Name of person), then (organization, title, or position)

Examples of this form include:

The institution learned that then men's volleyball student-athlete Ron Blocker was offered …
or
On March 1, 2003, Gail Resourceful, then assistant athletics director for compliance, interviewed …

NCAA Constitution and Bylaws

When referencing the NCAA Constitution or specific bylaws for the first time in a report, provide complete information on the provision in the body of the report. Generally, an indication of the year of the legislation is not needed in the text of a report. However, when the discussion deals with a version of the legislation from an earlier year or edition of the NCAA Manual, the date of the version of the bylaw referenced should be included in the citation. The basic forms are:

NCAA Constitution, constitution number-paragraph number, version of division manual (in parentheses)
or
Bylaw, bylaw number-paragraph number (version of division manual (in parentheses)

An example of this form:

The Division I Legislative Council used its authority set forth in NCAA Constitution 5.4.1.2.3 to reverse a previous council-approved official interpretation and agreed that a state- sponsored or private prepaid college tuition plan, purchased by a family member and paid to an institution on behalf of a student-athlete, is not considered aid from an outside source.

The committee notes that current legislation as set forth in NCAA Bylaws 12.02.4 and 12.1.1-(e) (2003-04 NCAA Division I Manual) imposes responsibilities on institutions additional to those imposed under legislation in effect at the time the case was processed.

Further, under Bylaw 12.1.1-(e) (2003-04 NCAA Division I Manual), "an individual loses his or her amateur status if the individual competes on any professional athletics team (per Bylaw 12.02.4), *even if no pay or remuneration for expenses was received"* (emphasis added).

During the summers of 2012 through 2014, the institution awarded athletically related financial aid to six prospective men's basketball student-athletes prior to their initial full-time enrollment in order for the young men to attend the institution's six-week summer program designed specifically and exclusively for first-time, first-year college students. NCAA Bylaws 13.2.1, 15.2.7, 15.2.7.1.2 (2013–14); 15.2.8 and 15.2.8.1.2 (2012–13 NCAA Division I Manual).

Legislative Proposals

NCAA legislation is added or revised through the passage of proposals by the division-specific boards of directors, presidents' councils, and management councils. If the body of the report is not clear as to which division the legislative proposal belongs, specify the division in the citation. The basic form is:

> Proposal No. (year-proposal number)
> *or*
> Division (I, II, or III) Proposal No. (year-proposal number)

An example of this form:

In an effort to facilitate and focus the membership's review of what the Academics/Eligibility/Compliance Cabinet and NCAA Division I Student-Athlete Advisory Committee (SAAC) has identified to the board of directors as a priority issue, the Academics/Eligibility/Compliance Cabinet modified its recommendation during its September meeting and recommended the NCAA Division I Management Council support Proposal No. 2002-83-A (financial aid—individual limit) ...

Decisions of the Infractions Committees

The NCAA committees on infractions and infractions appeals committees issue public reports on decisions regarding enforcement cases before them. The NCAA does not have an official reporter system but publishes public infractions and infractions appeals reports on the NCAA website (www. ncaa.org) and in the Legislative Services Database (LSDBi).

Committee on Infractions

The essential elements of the citation format for infractions reports issued by the committees on infractions consist of the name of the institution and the date of the issuance of the committee's report. If it is known, a good element in a citation is the infractions report or enforcement case number. (Infractions reports prior to 2000 and after 2013 do not consistently reference infractions or case numbers.) Other elements, including division, page numbers, and report date, are optional depending on the use of the reference in the document. For example, if a party is citing decisions of the Division II Committee on Infractions to a panel of the Division I Committee on Infractions, citations can be division-specific. After the first reference to a case, the short version of the citation may be used in the document. Finally, the Division I Committee on Infractions sometimes describes its reports as "infractions decisions"; thus, the citation for an infractions decision can use the term "decision" rather than "case" or "report". The basic forms are:

Name of institution (in italics), Case No. (decision number) at p. (page number), date of report (in parentheses)
or
Name of institution (in italics), Decision No. (decision number) at p. (page number), date of report (in parentheses)

Name of institution (in italics), Report No. (report number) at p. (page number), date of report (in parentheses)
or
Name of institution (in italics), Report at p. (page number), date of report (in parentheses)

Examples of this form include:

University of Georgia, Decision No. 413 at pp. 1-2 (December 16, 2014)

Auburn University, Report No. 219 at pp. 3–4 (April 27, 2004)

University of Arkansas at Pine Bluff, Report at p. 2 (November 5, 2014)

The committee concluded in a previous case that "the former president violated NCAA legislation relating to institutional control in that he did not ensure that all aspects of the athletic program were compliant with NCAA and institutional policies when he arranged for student-athlete A to be certified in a manner that was contrary to institutional policy." *Gardner-Webb University*, Report No. 217 at p. 3 (March 4, 2004).

The institution has modeled its initial eligibility program after this committee's findings in previous infractions cases. See *Morehouse College*, Report No. 213 at p. 6 (November 5, 2003). Specifically, the institution does not permit its intercollegiate athletic teams to be operated independently from the athletic department. *Morehouse College* at p. 6.

The committee has recently addressed cases involving violations of NCAA legislation relating to ethical conduct and academic fraud. *California State University, Northridge*, Report No. 220 (March 30, 2004).

In several recent cases, including the 2001 *Jacksonville University* case [Report No. 187 at p. 15 (August 30, 2001)], this committee has advised directors of athletics to report their concerns to appropriate officials at the respective conference office and/or the NCAA.

Infractions Appeals Committees

The essential elements of the citation format for reports issued by the infractions appeals committees consist of the name of the institution and the appeals committee's report number. Other elements, including division, page numbers, and date of the report, are optional depending on the use of the reference in the document. After the first reference to a case, the short version of the citation may be used in the document. The basic forms are:

Name of institution (in italics), Appeals Report No. (report number) at p. (page number), date of report (in parentheses)
or
Name of institution (in italics), Appeals Report No. (report number), date of report (in parentheses)

Examples of this form include:

Salem State College, Appeals Report No. 203 (August 28, 2003).

The institution notes that the infractions appeals committee has identified seven factors to be considered in the selection and application of penalties generally. See *University of Michigan*, Appeals Report No. 208 at p. 9 (September 25, 2003)]

Committee Chair or Staff Decision

During the processing of an infractions case (either prior to, during, or after a hearing or an oral argument), the committee chair, the chief hearing officer (for a panel of the Division I Committee on Infractions), the staff of the committees on infractions, or the staff of the infractions appeals committee will make decisions on issues or requests (e.g., extension of time, inclusion of information in the record). A reference to a specific page number should be included if the decision is more than one page and if it will help the reader locate the relevant text. Cite a decision by the committee or panel chair or a committee staff member acting alone under the authority provided by NCAA legislation or internal operating procedures using the following format:

Name of institution (in italics), Enforcement Case No. (case number), name of decision-maker, title of decision-maker: date of decision (in parentheses), unpublished decision (in parentheses)

or

Name of institution (in italics), Report No. (report number), name of decision-maker, title of decision-maker: date of decision (in parentheses), unpublished decision (in parentheses)

or

Name of institution (in italics), Appeals Report No. (report number), name of decision-maker, title of decision-maker: date of decision (in parentheses), unpublished decision (in parentheses)

Examples of this form include:

The institution notes the enforcement staff and the committee on infractions have permitted parties to supplement the committee record prior to and after a hearing. See *North-South-East-West University*, Enforcement Case No. 00111 (Jane Dough, director of enforcement: January 15, 2019) (email decision); *State University*, Report No. 999 (John Doe, chief hearing officer: October 1, 2020) (unpublished decision). Further, the Division II and III Committees on Infractions permitted involved individuals to add evidence to the record after a hearing to cure a possible fair-process violation. See *ACME University*, Report No. 990 at pp. 2–3 (Jane Dough, chair: September 1, 2019) (oral decision); *Galaxy College*, Report No. 990 at pp. 2–3 (Glory Hall, chair: September 1, 2019) (unpublished letter decision).

Secondary and Student-Athlete Reinstatement Cases

The essential elements of the citation format for secondary and student-athlete reinstatement cases consist of the case type, number, and date. The basic form is:

(Case type) Case No. (case number), date of case (in parentheses)

Examples of this form include:

The institution has previously processed secondary violations that are related to the subject of its investigation. See Secondary Case No. 9998 (January 15, 2003).

The student-athlete reinstatement staff has addressed the eligibility of the involved student-athlete. Eligibility Case No. 9999 (August 7, 2002).

Waiver Cases

The essential elements of the citation format for initial-eligibility, progress-toward-degree, and legislative relief waiver cases consist of the case type, number, and date. The basic form is:

(Waiver type) Waiver No. (waiver case number), date of waiver decision (in parentheses)

Examples of this form include:

The staff has approved similar waivers while noting the mitigating circumstances. See Initial-Eligibility Waiver No. 20935 (2010–11).

In accordance with the quality point analysis, student-athletes above a 50 percent chance of graduating within five years of enrollment at this point have been approved by the staff in recent years. See Progress-Toward Degree Waiver No. 6299 (September 9, 2010).

The Division I Legislative Council Subcommittee for Legislative Relief has granted a blanket waiver of the requirements in Bylaw 13.6.3-(c) and (d). See Legislative Relief Waiver No. 13911 (January 10, 2011).

Official and Unofficial Committee and Staff Interpretations and Educational Columns

The essential elements of the citation format for interpretations and educational columns issued by an NCAA body or staff should include sufficient information to identify the type of interpretation, the specific number of the interpretation, and issuance date. Other elements, including the interpreting body and division, are optional depending on the use of the reference in the document. The basic form is:

In brackets: AMA (interpretation type): title of interpretation; in parentheses: Issued and published: date of publication.

An example of this form:

The institution relied on an official interpretation in preparing this report. AMA Official Interpretation: "Providing benefits of nominal value to student-athletes who have exhausted eligibility" (Issued and published: January 6, 1989).

Letters, Memoranda, and Notes to the Investigative File

The basic citation form for letters, memoranda, and notes generated during an investigation should contain sufficient information to identify the type of document, the document's author, the recipient, and the date of the document. The subject matter of the document is optional. The basic form is:

Letter from (or "Memorandum from" or "Note from"), name and title of author to name and title of recipient, date (in parentheses), subject of item, if appropriate (in parentheses).

An example of this form includes:

The institution asserts that its senior administrators were diligent in performing their duties. Memorandum from Bob Snow, State University director of athletics, to Carroll Webb, State University chief executive officer (October 16, 1990) (explaining actions implemented by administrators to address issues discovered during September 25, 1990, compliance audit).

Transcripts, Audio Tapes, and Memoranda of Investigation Interviews

The basic citation form for an interview conducted for enforcement, student-athlete reinstatement, or other information-gathering purposes depends on the source (e.g., transcript, audiotape, or memorandum) being cited. If the interview tapes or notes are at a custodial site or are being maintained at the NCAA or at an institution, the location need not be included in a parenthetical clause. The title of the person being interviewed may be included if that would provide helpful information (for example, if the person has not previously been fully referenced in the document) and would not create a cluttered citation. After the first reference to an interview, the short version of the citation may be used. The basic forms are:

> Name of person interviewed date of interview interview transcript at p. (number or numbers)
>
> *or*
>
> Audiotape-recording of (date of interview) interview of (name of person interviewed), location of audiotape-recording of the interview, if helpful (in parentheses)
>
> *or*
>
> Memorandum (or Notes or Statement) of (date of interview) interview of (name of person interviewed) at p. (number or numbers), location of audiotape-recording of interview, if helpful (in parentheses)

Examples of this form include:

The institution notes, however, that only one student-athlete received an extra benefit from the athletic representative. Audiotape-recording of 3/15/03 interview of Jane Doe; Memorandum of 6/1/02 interview of John Doe at p. 2; John Doe 6/1/02 interview transcript at pp. 30–33.

Miscellaneous Citations

Citations and references to other materials and information in an infractions report can be prepared based on the report author's best judgment or adaption of other styles in nationally recognized publications (e.g., *The Bluebook*, APA citation style, MLA citation style, *The Chicago Manual of Style*).

CHAPTER 4

INVESTIGATION RESOURCES

NCAA Resources (as of June 30, 2014)_

The NCAA offers numerous resources and services to its member institutions and athletic conferences, including the following:

NCAA Website (www.ncaa.org). The NCAA website contains the most recent version of each division manual, infractions decisions, and other information.

Committees on Infractions. Telephone: +1-317-917-6222; website: www.ncaa.org; address: 700 West Washington Street; Indianapolis, Indiana 46206.

Enforcement Services Group. Telephone: +1-317-917-6222; website: www.ncaa.org; address: 700 West Washington Street, Indianapolis, Indiana 46206.

Books

In addition to the sources listed in the bibliography, the following books provide excellent summaries of investigative strategies and techniques for internal investigators:

Brian, Brad D. and Barry F. McNeil. *Internal Corporate Investigations (5310310).* 2nd ed. Chicago: American Bar Association, 2002.

Freedman, Warren. *Internal Company Investigations and the Employment Relationship.* New York: Quorum Books, 1994.

Propper, Eugene M. *Corporate Fraud Investigations & Compliance Programs.* St. Dobbs Ferry, New York: Oceana Publictions 2000.

Quay, John. *Diagnostic Interviewing for Consultants and Auditors: A Collaborative Approach to Problem Solving.* Cincinnati, Ohio: Quay Associates, 1994.

Weinberg, C. Donald. *Effective Interviewing and Interrogation Techniques.* San Diego, California: Academic Press, 2002.

Investigation Firm

Buckner. Contact: Michael L. Buckner. Telephone: +1-954-941-1844; facsimile: +1-954-941-1846; electronic mail: info@bucknersportslaw.

com; company website: http://www.bucknersportslaw.com; address: 7771 West Oakland Park Boulevard, Suite 162, Sunrise, Florida 33351.

Directories and Internet Resources

The following is a partial list of directories and Internet resources that provide information on a variety of topics:

Council of State Historical Records Coordinators (http://www.coshrc.org). The Council of State Historical Records Coordinators, a national organization made up of state historical records coordinators and their deputies, provides a directory of state archives and records programs.

Directories in Print (compiled by Gale Research International, Ltd.). This publication describes approximately 15,500 active rosters, guides, and other print and nonprint address lists published in the United States and worldwide. Hundreds of additional directories (defunct, suspended, or those that can no longer be located) are also cited with status notes in the title/keyword index.

Florida Association of Licensed Investigators (http://www.fali.org). The Florida Association of Licensed Investigators' website features a page containing links to databases, federal and state resources, magazines, newspapers, private investigator associations' websites (which contain other resources), and search engines.

Hi Tek's Investigative Resources (http://www.hitekinfo.com/links). Hi Tek's website provides links to hundreds of investigative resources.

Investigator's Toolbox: Resources for Researchers (http://www.virtuallibrarian.com/it/index.html). The Investigator's Toolbox website contains links to research resources, databases, and websites.

Legal Information Institute (http://www.law.cornell.edu/topics/index.html). The Legal Information Institute's "Law About" pages provide brief summaries of law topics with links to key primary source material, other Internet resources, and useful off-net references. The resources can be accessed through a set of broad topic categories, an alphabetical listing of topics, and a searchable index.

Lexis Database (http://www.lexis-nexis.com). LexisNexis provides authoritative legal, news, public records, and business information, including tax and regulatory publications in online, print, or CD-ROM formats.

Martindale-Hubbell Law Directory (http://martindale.com). Martindale-Hubbell is the authoritative resource for information on the worldwide legal profession.

VirtualGumshoe.com (http://www.virtualgumshoe.com/resources). The website has an excellent directory of free public records databases and resources.

Westlaw Database (http://www.westlaw.com). Westlaw is an online legal research service. It provides quick, easy access to West's vast collection of statutes, case law materials, public records, and other legal resources, along with current news articles and business information.

PART 4

GUIDE TO COMMITTEE ON INFRACTIONS PROCEDURAL DECISIONS

This section reviews decisions of the NCAA committees on infractions and infractions appeals committees for all three divisions (through December 31, 2014) that address evidentiary and procedural issues. The term *committee on infractions*, when used in this section, refers to the committee on infractions and committee hearing panels in Division I and the committees on infractions in Divisions II and III. The term *infractions appeals committee*, when used in this section, refers to the appeals committees in Divisions I, II, and III. The applicable infractions decisions relating to an issue are cited in italics.

Note: The text contains citations of the 2014–15 NCAA Divisions I, II, and III manuals. Readers are encouraged to refer to the NCAA website, www.ncaa.org, for the most recent legislative revisions, additions, and adjustments.

Absence from Hearing Room—Committee Members

The reliability of the evidence relied on by the committee on infractions is affected by the absence of a committee member from the hearing room only if the record demonstrates: (a) "when or for how long the Committee on Infractions committee member was absent from the hearing"; and (b) "the member's absence constituted reversible procedural error" because the member was not sufficiently informed on the issues that were discussed when the member was absent from the room. *Southeast Missouri State University, Former Head Men's Basketball Coach*, Appeals Report No. 302 at p. 5 (June 25, 2010).

Abuse of Discretion (See Penalties—Abuse of Discretion)

Adequate Notice

The principle of fair process requires the enforcement staff, the committees on infractions and the infractions appeals committees to provide institutions and involved individuals with adequate notice of allegations as well as procedural decisions that have an adverse impact on a party. *University of Louisville, Assistant Men's Basketball Coach*, Appeals Report No. 154 at pp. 5–6 (September 22, 1998). For example, in the *University of Louisville, Assistant Men's Basketball Coach* appeals case, the Division I Infractions

111

Appeals Committee determined that an involved individual was not "provided adequate notice that the Committee on Infractions considered his alleged violations to be major violations. The procedural error affected the reliability of the information upon which the findings were based." *University of Louisville, Assistant Men's Basketball Coach* at p. 5. Further, the appeals committee held the "lack of adequate notice was a serious procedural error in this case which disadvantaged the institution [since] it prevented the University from advancing its analysis and arguments that the violations were secondary." *University of Louisville, Assistant Men's Basketball Coach* at p. 6.

Affidavits

The Division I Infractions Appeals Committee does not believe affidavits are "the most effective way to resolve factual disputes." *University at Buffalo, the State University of New York, Former Head Men's Basketball Coach*, Appeals Report No. 181 at p. 7 (October 12, 2001). Instead, the appeals committee notes "it is far more helpful for the NCAA enforcement staff to interview witnesses having relevant information so that they can be asked all relevant questions about the circumstances involved." *University at Buffalo, the State University of New York, Former Head Men's Basketball Coach* at p. 7. However, the Division I Committee on Infractions determines the probative value of an affidavit based on three factors: (a) whether the affidavit was notarized or otherwise affirmed by the executing party; (b) whether the affidavit was specifically prepared for purposes of an infractions hearing; and (c) whether the affidavit was in conflict with prior statements made by the executing party during the investigation. *University of Connecticut*, Report No. 339 at p. 3 (February 22, 2011). The committee's rationale appears to discourage parties from submitting self-serving affidavits and to encourage the development of evidence that has been subjected to a minimal level of cross-examination.

Appeals—Notice of Appeal

NCAA legislation and the published internal procedures for the infractions appeals committees provide guidelines for the eligibility, initiation, and processing of an appeal of a decision by the committee on infractions. A party perfects an appeal by submitting a timely notice of appeal and by filing a written appeal that provides "the Infractions Appeals Committee with sufficient information to properly frame the issues for consideration," including procedural errors and other issues described in NCAA legislation. *Gonzaga University, Former Director of Athletics*, Appeals Report No. 152 at p. 5 (July 30, 1998); *Alabama A&M University, Former Head Soccer Coach*, Appeals Report No. 129 at p. 4 (October 11, 1996).

Appeals (Summary Disposition)—Proposed Penalties

After a committee on infractions or hearing panel's review of a summary disposition report, a party may contest a committee's or panel's proposed penalties at an expedited hearing. *University of Arkansas at Pine Bluff*, Report at p. 1 (November 5, 2014). Following an expedited hearing, a party "has the opportunity to appeal those penalties" under the procedure articulated in Bylaws 19 (for Division I) and 32 (for Divisions II and III). *University of Arkansas at Pine Bluff* at p. 1.

Appearance of an Involved Individual at a Hearing or an Oral Argument

NCAA legislation and the published internal committee on infractions and infractions appeals committee procedures permit involved individuals to be represented by legal counsel at an infractions hearing or an oral argument. The legislation and internal committee procedures do not permit an involved individual's legal counsel to appear at an infractions hearing or an oral argument alone (i.e., without the presence of the involved individual). *University of Minnesota–Twin Cities, Former Head Men's Basketball Coach*, Appeals Report No. 176 at p. 10 (October 24, 2000). The Division I Infractions Appeals Committee, in the *University of Minnesota–Twin Cities, Former Head Men's Basketball Coach* appeals case, ruled that "an institution by its nature can 'appear' only by sending representatives," but "this rationale [does not apply] to individual respondents." *University of Minnesota–Twin Cities, Former Head Men's Basketball Coach* at p. 10. For example, an involved individual cannot make an appearance by sending legal counsel alone, even if the party was "unwilling to appear at the hearing because of a pending criminal investigation (an indirect reference, we assume, to his unwillingness to risk that his testimony at the hearing might be used against him in a subsequent criminal proceeding)." *University of Minnesota–Twin Cities, Former Head Men's Basketball Coach* at p. 10.

The Division III Committee on Infractions, in the *College of Staten Island* case, did not permit the legal counsel for a head coach to participate in an infractions hearing without the presence of the coach. *College of Staten Island*, Report No. 395 at p. 2 (November 21, 2013). However, the committee on infractions may use its discretion to permit an involved individual to appear at an infractions hearing through legal counsel alone if the involved individual is unable to attend the proceeding due to physical circumstances (e.g., hospitalization for a severe medical condition). *Texas A&M University–Corpus Christi*, Report No. 298 (March 25, 2009) (unpublished ruling).

Clerical Errors

Clerical errors by the committees on infractions can serve as a basis for an appeal. *University of Michigan*, Appeals Report No. 208 at p. 8 (September 25, 2003).

Conflict of Interest—Committee Members

NCAA legislation prohibits a member of a committee on infractions (Division I Bylaw 19.3.4 and Divisions II and III Bylaw 32.1.3) or the infractions appeals committee (Division I Bylaw 19.4.3 and Divisions II and III Bylaw 32.1.3) from participating in a case if the member is directly connected with an institution under investigation or if the member has a personal, professional, or institutional affiliation that may create the appearance of partiality. Under the rules, the panel or committee member has the responsibility to remove himself or herself if a conflict exists. A party's objection to the participation of a panel or committee member in a case "should be raised as soon as recognized but will not be considered unless raised at least one week in advance" of the panel's or appeals committee's review of the case. Division I Bylaw 19.3.4 notes a party's "objections will be decided by the committee chair" in instances involving a panel of the committee on infractions. According to case precedent, a party waives an objection if the party knew of the pertinent facts prior to a hearing or an oral argument but failed to raise an objection within the time limit imposed by NCAA legislation. *Missouri State University, Former Head Men's Basketball Coach*, Appeals Report No. 302 at p. 5 (June 25, 2010). However, if a party learned of facts suggesting a conflict existed with a member of the committee on infractions only after the issuance of a committee report, the party is obligated to present such information to the committee on infractions. *Missouri State University, Former Head Men's Basketball Coach* at p. 5.

Due Process (See Fair Process)

Evidence—Accuracy and Completeness

All parties—the enforcement staff, the institution, and involved individuals—participating in the enforcement process are obligated to provide the committee on infractions with complete information. The accuracy and completeness of the evidence presented to the committee on infractions is not affected if an involved individual is denied the opportunity to be present at, and to participate in, interviews of witnesses by the institution or the enforcement staff. *Stetson University, Former Head Men's Basketball Coach*, Appeals Report No. 195 at p. 10 (December 13, 2002). Instead, the institution and involved individual can influence the accuracy and completeness of the record through several methods: (a) the institution and involved individual are provided opportunities to review the enforcement staff's investigative file; and (b) parties are permitted to provide a more comprehensive presentation of the evidence developed during the investigation if the party concludes the enforcement staff's submission is not accurate or complete. *Stetson University, Former Head Men's Basketball Coach* at p. 10.

Further, a party's "failure to make a timely delivery of the documents" constitutes a "failure to cooperate" since it prevents the enforcement staff from posing questions concerning the documents or to follow up on relevant information. *University of North Carolina, Chapel Hill*, Report No. 360 at pp. 15–16 (March 12, 2012). However, a committee on infractions has the discretion to conclude an involved individual did not refuse to cooperate by failing to provide information when requested by the enforcement staff when the individual: (a) first refused to provide the records citing privacy concerns; (b) subsequently agreed to provide the records; and (c) made a good faith effort in obtaining the records (for example, initially encountered difficulties in obtaining the correct records from a third party, but later securing the pertinent records). *Henderson State University*, Report at pp. 25-26 (July 29, 2014). Further, "in making this conclusion, the committee [can take] into consideration the fact" the involved individual "was initially not provided access to all of the records pertinent to the allegations in which he [or she] was named". *Henderson State University* at pp. 25-26. In such instances, the committee has the discretion to provide an involved individual with an additional period from the close of the hearing to submit a supplemental response or information previously requested by the enforcement staff. *Henderson State University* at pp. 2-3.

Evidence—Credibility Determination

Under NCAA legislation, the committee on infractions makes "determinations regarding matters such as relevance, credibility and the sufficiency of the information presented to it." *University of Mississippi*, Appeals Report No. 111 at p. 8 (November 17, 1994); *Jacksonville University, Former Soccer Coach*, Appeals Report No. 187 at p. 8 (March 22, 2002). On the other hand, it is not within the purview of the infractions appeals committee to make determinations of fact or to assess the credibility of witnesses. *Salem State University*, Appeals Report No. 203 at p. 8 (August 28, 2003).

Evidence—New Evidence

NCAA legislation and case precedent define *new evidence* as: (a) relevant, material information that could not have reasonably been ascertained prior to the committee on infractions hearing; and (b) information related, directly or indirectly, to any of the findings of the case. *Purdue University, Former Assistant Basketball Coach*, Appeals Report No. 193 at p. 9 (September 17, 2002); *Albany State University*, Appeals Report No. 170 at p. 12 (March 9, 2000). The committee on infractions could consider a document as new evidence if the information meets the bylaw definition and its exclusion from the case would be prejudicial to an institution or an involved individual. For example, the infractions appeals committee ruled that because three letters involving eligibility matters, provided by an institution to enforcement staff during an investigation, were not brought to the attention of the committee on infractions, they were not considered new evidence. *University of Texas at El Paso*, Appeals Report No. 140 at p. 6 (January 7, 1998).

New evidence also does not include: (a) information provided by institutional administrators after a hearing or an oral argument if the statements "do not concern evidence related to any findings" in the case; (b) a letter from a former institutional employee who served as the institution's spokesperson during the hearing; or (c) information related to corrective actions taken by an institution after a hearing. *Texas State University-San Marcos, Former Head Baseball Coach*, Appeals Committee Report No. 110 at p. 4 (November 3, 1994); *University of Texas at El Paso*, Appeals Report No. 140 at p. 6 (January 7, 1998).

If an institution or involved individual appeals findings of major violations or penalties, a showing of new evidence directly related to the findings in the case that is discovered during the appeals process must be referred back to the committee on infractions for review. *Albany State University*, Appeals Report No. 170 at p. 11 (March 9, 2000). To appeal the committee on infractions' denial of information as new evidence, a party must ensure that the request to the committee to consider new evidence is clear on the record. *Ball State University, Former Head Women's Tennis Coach*, Appeals Report No. 326 at p. 11 (April 27, 2011).

Evidence—Rules of Evidence

NCAA enforcement proceedings are not judicial proceedings. *University of Mississippi*, Appeals Report No. 111 at pp. 7–8 (November 17, 1994). Accordingly, the infractions appeals committee has explained that "formal rules of evidence are not applicable; testimony is not taken under oath; the Committee on Infractions, when it finds a violation, does not issue specific findings of fact; the committee is not required to consider the weight of the evidence (i.e., whether, and to what extent, the evidence supporting the finding of a violation outweighs evidence to the contrary)." *University of*

Mississippi at pp. 7–8. Instead, NCAA legislation requires the committee on infractions to base its findings on information presented to it that meets the criteria specified in Division I Bylaw 19 and Divisions II and III Bylaws 19 and 32. See *University of Mississippi* at pp. 7–8.

Evidence—Ten- and Thirty-Day Deadline Submission

NCAA legislation (Division I Bylaw 19.7.5 and Divisions II and III Bylaw 32.6.8) requires that all written material from parties to be considered by the committee on infractions must be received by the committee, enforcement staff, institution, and any involved individuals at least thirty days in Division I and at least ten days in Divisions II and III prior to the hearing date. However, the committee (or the chief hearing officer in Division I) has discretion to admit evidence after the deadline or at the hearing; the committee may exclude information that it determines to be irrelevant, immaterial, or unduly repetitious. (See Division I Bylaw 19.7.7.3 and Divisions II and III Bylaw 32.8.7.4). However, the committee on infractions' failure to admit evidence submitted after the deadline is not an abuse of discretion. *California State University, Northridge, Former Assistant Men's Basketball Coach,* Appeals Report No. 220 at p. 9 (October 28, 2004).

Exculpatory Evidence

Exculpatory evidence consists of evidence that favors an involved individual in an infractions hearing and can be used to establish the individual's innocence. The enforcement staff's alleged failure to "adequately develop potentially exculpatory information" (based on "alleged inadequacies in the nature of the questions posed to individuals who provided information to the NCAA and the institution") is not an error when "the allegedly inconsistent statements" that "should have been challenged by the enforcement staff were presented to the Committee on Infractions." *Ohio State University, Division I Former Assistant Men's Basketball Coach's Appeal,* Report No. 256 at p. 9 (April 13, 2007).

Failure to Monitor (Head Coach)—No Requirement of Supporting Underlying Violation

A head coach failure to monitor finding does not have to be supported by an underlying violation when the committee on infractions concludes the coach "acted contrary to institutional policy and contrary to the advice and caution provided by" institutional staff. *University of Georgia*, Decision No. 413 at pp. 10-11 (December 16, 2014). Further, a failure to monitor finding is appropriate, even if "an advantage did not result from the head coach's violations", but the record demonstrates the coach's "actions were intended to create more than a minimal competitive advantage and it involved conduct that could have undermined and threatened the integrity of the NCAA Collegiate Model." *University of Georgia* at p. 2.

Fair Process

An institution and involved individual have a right to a fair process during enforcement procedures. The NCAA's obligations do not rise to a due process standard. Specifically, federal and state courts require voluntary associations, clubs, and groups to establish and maintain fair procedures to govern the treatment or regulation of members and nonmembers. See *Silver v. New York Stock Exchange*, 373 U.S. 341, 358-61 (1963); *Ezekial v. Winkley*, 20 Cal. 3d 267, 271–72 (Cal. 1977). The NCAA violates a party's fair process rights when an enforcement-related procedure, decision, or action is arbitrary (substantively unreasonable, internally irregular, and procedurally unfair). See *Ezekial v. Winkley*, 20 Cal. 3d 267, 271–72 (Cal. 1977). For example, an involved individual is not denied fair or due process when the committee on infractions finds a violation that had not been alleged by the enforcement staff based on information developed or discussed during the hearing. *Purdue University, Former Assistant Basketball Coach*, Appeals Report No. 193 at p. 4 (September 17, 2002). However, a procedural error occurs when the enforcement staff fails "to meet its obligations to carry out its investigation" with a commitment to fairness of procedures as well as the timely and equitable resolution of an infractions case. *West Virginia University, Former Head Men's Soccer Coach*, Appeal Report No. 265 at p. 10 (April 4, 2008).

Michael L. Buckner

False Information

An involved individual can be cited for unethical conduct and other violations if he or she "knowingly" instructs a person "to provide false and misleading information" to the enforcement staff, institutional investigators, or the committee on infractions. *University of Central Oklahoma*, Appeals Report No. 283 at 2 (August 6, 2008).

Hearing Spokesperson

An institution selects one person to serve as its principal spokesperson during a hearing. Generally, "an institution is bound by the statements its representatives make at NCAA infractions hearings. Once those comments have gone unchallenged at the hearing, the institution is bound by them absent contrary evidence produced at the hearing or later by newly discovered evidence." *University of Texas at El Paso*, Appeals Report No. 140 at p. 7 (January 7, 1998). In fact, an institution is bound by the principle spokesperson's statements, even if the comments were unsubstantiated, derived from personal observations and anecdotal information, or were not based on reliable evidence developed during the investigation if the institution "failed to challenge these comments at the hearing." *University of Texas at El Paso* at p. 7.

Hearing Record

The record of an infractions hearing includes the notice of allegations, the parties' responses to the notice of allegations, the hearing transcript, and other evidence declared as such by the committee on infractions. A finding by the committee on infractions must be based on information contained in the hearing record. *Albany State University*, Appeals Report No. 170 at p. 13 (March 9, 2000); *MacMurray College*, Appeals Report No. 235 at p. 8 (February 3, 2006).

Inaccurate Transcript

Errors "prejudicial" to a party's case in the hearing transcript can form the basis for an extension of the deadline to submit, or make changes to, an appellate document. *University of Texas at El Paso*, Appeals Report No. 140 at p. 5 (January 7, 1998).

Inadmissible Information

An interview memorandum not signed by a witness can be considered inadmissible evidence at the hearing by the committee on infractions. *Purdue University*, Appeals Report No. 134 at p. 12 (January 25, 2000).

Institutional Violations—Nexus with Underlying Violation

The committee on infractions creates reversible error if its finding of an institutional violation (e.g., lack of institutional control, failure to monitor) does not have a "nexus" with the underlying violation. *University of Oklahoma*, Appeals Report No. 270 at pp. 6–7 (February 22, 2008). For example, a nexus does not exist between a failure to monitor for violations and an underlying rules violation when the conduct that formed the basis of the underlying finding did not constitute an NCAA rules violation. *University of Oklahoma* at pp. 6–7.

Investigations—Complete Investigations by the Enforcement Staff

The enforcement staff is required to conduct a complete investigation. However, according to the committee on infractions, "it is true in every case that additional witnesses could be interviewed," but "there is no requirement that the enforcement representatives interview additional witnesses if in their judgment they have gathered sufficient evidence to make a case to the Committee on Infractions." *Southeast Missouri State University, Former Head Men's Basketball Coach*, Report No. 150 at p. 4 (January 11, 1999). Instead, the committee says involved individuals (with the assistance of legal counsel) have "the opportunity to interview individuals" in a case and have "the burden to bring forth evidence favorable" to their position and "cannot discharge this duty by alleging that the enforcement representatives should have produced this evidence." *Southeast Missouri State University, Former Head Men's Basketball Coach* at p. 4.

Lack of Adequate Notice

The NCAA enforcement staff and infractions committees are obligated, under the principle of fair process, to provide parties with "adequate notice" of procedures, decisions, and other actions. A failure to provide adequate notice can constitute a procedural error that can form the basis for a vacation of a finding if the error affected the reliability of the information used by the committee on infractions to support a finding. *University of California, Los Angeles, Former Senior Associate Director of Athletics*, Appeals Report No. 141 at p. 17 (November 7, 1997); *University of Alabama*, Appeals Report No. 120 at p. 7 (November 30, 1995); see also *University at Buffalo, State University of New York, Former Head Coach's Appeal*, Appeals Report No. 181 at p. 8 (October 12, 2001).

Notice of Allegations—Failure to Respond

The committee on infractions deems any allegation against an institution or involved individual as admitted if a response to the charge is not filed or received by the committee. *University of Southern Mississippi*, Report at p. 9 (January 30, 2013).

Objections during a Hearing

The infraction process follows the "uniform rule that if one wishes to object on appeal to a matter which has taken place during a trial or administrative hearing, the objection must first be raised at the trial or hearing. The purpose of such an objection is to permit the judge or hearing officer to consider whether the proposed action is improper. To do otherwise would permit the participants at a hearing to allow an error to occur and then raise that error for the first time on appeal." *Florida State University*, Appeals Report No. 128 at p. 10 (October 1, 1996).

Penalties

The committee on infractions possesses the authority to conclude whether violations of the NCAA Constitution or bylaws occurred and, if so, to determine appropriate penalties. The committee can provide an institution or involved individual with relief from the penalties if the record demonstrates the existence of mitigating factors. *Texas Southern University*, Report at p. 21 (October 9, 2012); *California State University, Northridge, Former Assistant Men's Basketball Coach's Appeal*, Appeal Report No. 220 at p. 10 (October 28, 2004). The infractions appeals committee can evaluate the committee on infractions' analysis of the penalties imposed in a case on appeal when compared with the penalties imposed "in other cases with similar characteristics as an additional factor that it deems significant in considering an appeal of penalties." *University of Mississippi*, Appeals Report No. 111 at p. 11 (May 1, 1995).

Penalties—Abuse of Discretion

A penalty prescribed by the committee on infractions, including determinations regarding the existence and weighing of any aggravating or mitigating factors, shall not be set aside on appeal except on a showing by the appealing party that the committee abused its discretion. An abuse of discretion in the imposition of a penalty occurs if the penalty: (a) was not based on a correct legal standard or was based on a misapprehension of the underlying substantive legal principles; (b) was based on a clearly erroneous factual finding; (c) failed to consider and weigh material factors; (d) was based on a clear error of judgment such that the imposition was arbitrary, capricious, or irrational; or (e) was based in significant part on one or more irrelevant or improper factors (the "Alabama State University standard"). *Alabama State University*, Appeals Report No. 289 at p. 23 (June 30, 2009). Further, in Division II, abuse of discretion includes penalties that are "excessive." *University of Southern Indiana*, Report No. 331 at p. 4 (October 4, 2011).

For example, under the Alabama State University standard, the committee on infractions abuses its discretion when, in cases involving multiple sports, it fails to "clearly delineate the factors associated with the penalties for each sport when multiple circumstances and disparate behavior are before the Committee on Infractions." *University of Central Florida*, Appeals Report No. 372 at pp. 13–14 (April 22, 2013). Further, the committee on infractions abuses its discretion in fashioning penalties when it fails to "adequately distinguish" between the factors on which postseason bans are based. *University of Central Florida* at pp. 13–14. For example, the rationale for a postseason penalty in one sport cannot be "so intricately woven with factors only supportive" of the postseason penalty in a second sport "as to make it impossible to determine whether these additional factors formed a significant basis for the Committee on Infractions imposition" of the first sport's postseason penalty "in addition to the full range of other significant penalties placed on the" first sport's program specifically and the institution overall. *University of Central Florida* at pp. 13–14. Further, the committee on infractions is obligated to "make it clear the extent to which the finding of a lack of institutional control is based on the infractions in" one sport as opposed to the infractions in a second sport, if applicable. *University of Central Florida* at pp. 13–14.

The committee on infractions also abuses its discretion when it imposes a postseason penalty that "is inconsistent and excessive relative to the overall circumstances presented." *University of Central Florida* at pp. 13–14. For example, an error occurs if a penalty appears inconsistent with the disparities in conduct and material factors applicable to a sports program. *University of Central Florida* at pp. 13–14.

In addition, the committee on infractions' imposition of a postseason ban does not require any of the factors enumerated in the applicable legislation to be present; instead, the committee may apply a postseason ban when any one factor is shown and when it "clearly articulates those factors" in the infractions report. *University of Central Florida* at pp. 13–14. However, "when the record creates the appearance that the Committee on Infractions relied on material factors not present for a particular sport to assess the penalty and there is no evidence in the record that the Committee on Infractions weighed the potential absence of those factors in its determination," the committee abuses "its discretion by failing to appropriately consider and weigh material factors." *University of Central Florida* at pp. 13–14.

Penalties—Application of New Division I Structure

The NCAA Division I Board of Directors enacted a new infractions process that became effective October 30, 2012. However, in cases involving violations that occurred prior to October 30, the committee on infractions hearing panel will conduct "a separate analysis" and make "a separate determination as to whether to prescribe penalties under the former NCAA or current NCAA Bylaw 19 penalty guidelines." *University of New Hampshire*, Report at p. 9 (June 27, 2014); *Howard University*, Report No. 405 at p. 14 (May 20, 2014). In such cases, the committee will select the penalty guidelines that are "more lenient." *University of New Hampshire* at p. 9; *Howard University* at p. 14. However, in instances when violations occurred over an extended period (e.g., four years) and the institution is a repeat violator, the hearing panel has the discretion to apply the new penalty guidelines. *University of New Hampshire* at p. 9.

Penalties—Self-Imposed Penalties

An institution and involved individual can self-impose a sanction and propose that the committee on infractions adopt the penalty. An institution also can self-impose the penalty of probation. The infractions appeals committee has recognized "that self-imposed probation does not carry with it the public force of probation imposed by the NCAA through a Committee on Infractions decision. In addition, the substantive provisions of self-imposed probation will vary, and there is no inherent process by which an institution's compliance with its terms can be verified or monitored by an external entity." *Alabama State University*, Appeals Report No. 289 at p. 25 (June 30, 2009). However, in cases where the record contains evidence that "there was widespread public knowledge of the self-imposed probation, its substantive elements were substantial, and the institution reported the status of its compliance with those elements to the NCAA through the enforcement staff" and to the institution's conference office, the self-imposed probation carries "with it the same operative elements and substantive deterrent effects as probation imposed by the NCAA, including its availability for use against the institution in recruiting by other institutions." *Alabama State University* at p. 25. Thus, in such instances, the committee on infractions' failure to "appropriately consider and weigh" a self-imposed probation "constitutes an abuse of discretion within the meaning of the test" articulated in the Alabama State University appeals case. *Alabama State University* at p. 25.

The committee on infractions can conclude an institution "had taken the position that no additional penalties were warranted in this case" if the institution did not propose any penalties in the summary disposition report. *University of New Hampshire*, Report at p. 3 (June 27, 2014).

Rules education is a corrective rather than punitive measure. *University of New Hampshire* at p. 3.

Penalties—Summary Disposition Proposed Penalties (See Appeals (Summary Disposition)—Proposed Penalties)

Prior Submission of Level III, Level IV, and Secondary Violations

The committee on infractions possesses discretion to consider (and impose additional sanctions concerning) a violation previously submitted by an institution as a breach of conduct (Level III violation) or incidental infraction (Level IV violation) in Division I or a secondary violation in Divisions II and III. Specifically, a committee's finding on a previously discovered and submitted Level III, Level IV, or secondary violation does not create "double jeopardy" for the institution. *Arizona State University*, Appeals Report No. 332 at p. 15–16 (December 15, 2010). The committee's review of information filed by the institution with the secondary enforcement staff or the conference office, or the discovery of additional evidence during the major enforcement case, can indicate that a previously submitted Level III or IV violation should be reclassified. *Arizona State University* at p. 15–16.

Reliability/Credibility of Information

The committee on infractions' findings must be supported by credible information. However, a procedural error that affects the reliability of the information used to support the committee on infractions' finding can form a basis for appeal. *New Mexico State University, Former Assistant Basketball Coach*, Appeals Report No. 130 at p. 5 (December 20, 1996); see also *Purdue University*, Appeals Report No. 134 at p. 11 (January 25, 2000); *Jacksonville University, Former Head Men's Soccer Coach*, Appeals Report No. 187 at p. 8 (March 22, 2002); *Howard University, Former Head Women's Basketball Coach*, Appeals Report No. 175 at p. 7 (July 16,

2002). However, the party making the contention that a procedural error affected the reliability of the information "has the burden to bring forth evidence favorable to [his or her] position and cannot discharge this duty by" making unsupported allegations. *Southeast Missouri State University, Former Head Men's Basketball Coach*, Appeals Report No. 150 at p. 4 (January 11, 1999).

The Division I Infractions Appeal Committee, in the *University of Alabama, Tuscaloosa*, appeals case, held that procedural error allegedly affecting the reliability of information did not occur when the committee on infractions cited evidence received from a confidential source if: (a) the identity of the source was disclosed to the institution; (b) the institution had the opportunity to interview the individual and judge the individual's credibility; and (c) the institution agreed to allow the enforcement staff to use evidence from the confidential source and submitted a letter waiving its rights under then Bylaw 32.7.5.5.1 (now Bylaw 19.7.7.3.1 in Division I). *University of Alabama, Tuscaloosa*, Appeals Report No. 193 at p. 16 (September 17, 2002).

Repeat-Violator Provision

The repeat-violator provision is automatic; the enforcement staff, the committee on infractions, and any other entity does not have "the authority to ignore its application" even if the enforcement staff contends it "should not be applied" in a case or no member of the committee on infractions comments on the provision during the hearing. *University of Texas at El Paso*, Appeals Report No. 140 at p. 9 (January 7, 1998).

Right to Counsel

Involved individuals have the right to legal counsel during all phases of the enforcement process, including during an interview conducted by the enforcement staff. Thus a procedural error occurs when the enforcement staff notifies an involved individual of the right to counsel but improperly threatens the party with a charge of failure to cooperate if the party asks "to adjourn the interview after it began in order to obtain counsel." *West Virginia University, Former Head Men's Soccer Coach*, Appeals Report No. 265 at p. 10 (April 4, 2008).

Standard of Proof

After an infractions hearing, the hearing panel (Division I) or the committee on infractions (Divisions II and III) deliberates in private and determines: (a) what findings should be made, if any; and (b) what penalties should be assessed, if any. The committee bases its decisions concerning violations on information deemed to be "credible, persuasive and of a kind on which reasonably prudent persons rely in the conduct of serious affairs." (See Division I Bylaw 19.7.8.3 and Divisions II and III Bylaw 32.8.8.2). The infractions committees have not defined the standard of proof. However, during "The Enforcement Experience," a 2011 NCAA presentation for media members, former Division I Committee on Infractions chair Josephine Potuto said the standard of proof can be defined as akin to the "clear and convincing evidence" standard used in civil court. Further, Potuto explained that each piece of evidence presented during an infractions hearing does not need to meet the standard; conversely, the infractions committee "can evaluate the totality of the evidence and then judge whether it has crossed that threshold" (Dodd 2011; Solomon 2011; Davis 2011).

Standing

Standing can be described as the interest an institution or involved individual has in a dispute or issue that entitles the institution or individual to bring the controversy before the committee on infractions or infractions appeals committee to obtain administrative relief. See *Gonzaga University, Former Director of Athletics*, Appeals Report No. 152 at p. 5 (July 30, 1998). For example, the Division I Infractions Appeals Committee, in the *Gonzaga University, Former Director of Athletics* appeals case, ruled a former director of athletics had standing to appeal a lack of institutional control finding made against the person's former institution; the former director of athletics declined to appeal the ruling. *Gonzaga University, Former Director of Athletics* at p. 5. The infractions appeals committee permitted "the appeal to proceed because the actions of the former director of athletics so permeated the finding of lack of institutional control in this case." *Gonzaga University, Former Director of Athletics* at p. 5. If the party is not provided the minimum levels of fair process, "any unethical conduct finding based on that conduct is procedural error." *Gonzaga University, Former Director of Athletics* at p. 5. An institution does not have standing to appeal a finding of unethical conduct made against a former coach and not the institution itself. *University of Southern California*, Appeals Report No. 323 at p. 22 (May 26, 2011).

Testimony of Witnesses

The testimony of witnesses can be a persuasive form of evidence during the infractions process. The committee on infractions determines the credibility of witnesses and whether their testimony should be relied on in the case. *New Mexico State University, Assistant Men's Basketball Coach*, Appeals Report No. 185 at p. 5 (June 20, 2001); *Florida State University*, Appeals Report No. 128 at p. 10 (October 1, 1996); *University of Southern California, Former Assistant Football Coach*, Appeals Report No. 323 at p. 8, 11 (April 29, 2011). However, the infractions appeals committee cautions "that matters decided by the Committee on Infractions may not be insulated from review simply by denominating them 'credibility determinations.'" *University of Southern California, Former Assistant Football Coach* at p. 11.

The committee on infractions may request the attendance of designated individuals, including former students, to provide testimony during an infractions hearing. NCAA legislation does not contain a restriction "on the authority of the Committee on Infractions to permit the attendance of additional witnesses when it deems it necessary or appropriate to do so," including "testimony from individuals not directly affiliated with an institution" (e.g., a coach's wife testifying as a character reference, and expert witnesses). *Florida State University* at p. 10.

An institution is provided adequate notice of an appearance by a witness if it is notified or aware of the possibility with the release of the notice of allegations (or provided an opportunity to request an extension from the committee). The "time frame allows ample opportunity to discuss and consider questions (e.g., who will appear at the hearing)." *Florida State University* at p. 10.

The committee on infractions does not commit procedural error by failing to provide an institution with "an opportunity to cross-examine or summon rebuttal witnesses" since committee hearings "are not formal judicial trials" and "there is no cross-examination of witnesses as there would be at a trial." *Florida State University* at p. 10. Instead, NCAA legislation specifies that the committee at its discretion shall question representatives of the member institution or the enforcement staff, as well as any other persons appearing before it, to determine the facts of the case. Further, questions and information may be exchanged among all parties participating in the infractions hearing through questions proposed by one party and, if approved, directed by the committee to another party or parties. *Florida State University* at p. 10.

Testimony from an interview is inadmissible in a hearing if the "enforcement staff did not tape record the interview because the witness appeared nervous" and "the witness subsequently refused to sign a memorandum of the interview." *Purdue University*, Appeals Report No. 134 at p. 12 (January 25, 2000). The enforcement staff does not commit procedural error when it relies "on statements from interviews conducted during the university's investigation," but the enforcement staff must satisfy "due diligence" by making "every effort to locate and interview relevant witnesses." *New Mexico State University, Assistant Men's Basketball Coach*, Appeals Report No. 185 at p. 5 (June 20, 2001).

Unethical Conduct

An involved individual charged with unethical conduct must be provided notice and "an opportunity to be heard on the question of his conduct during the investigation." *Indiana University, Bloomington, Former Assistant Coach A*, Supplemental Report No. M285 at p. 3 (February 20, 2009).

Waiver of Rights

If an institution waives its rights afforded by NCAA legislation "on a limited or conditional basis, it must articulate those conditions in its waiver." *University of Alabama, Tuscaloosa*, Appeals Report No. 193 at p. 16 (September 17, 2002).

Web Custodial

NCAA Bylaw 19.5.9 requires the enforcement staff to provide the member institution and all involved individuals "recorded interviews, interview summaries and/or interview transcripts, and other factual information pertinent to the case. The institution and involved individuals may review such information through a secure website or at the NCAA national office." *Purdue University, Former Assistant Basketball Coach*, Appeals Report No. 193 at p. 8 (September 17, 2002). Generally, protocol dictates that the enforcement staff provides access to the web custodial site within several business days after the issuance of the notice of allegations. However, a party may be prejudiced if the enforcement staff fails to provide access to the site, or to documents on it, within a reasonable time. *Purdue University, Former Assistant Basketball Coach* at p. 8. The committee on infractions has concluded prejudice exists if a party "was denied 'reasonable access' to these materials." *Purdue University, Former Assistant Basketball Coach* at p. 8. The Division II Committee on Infractions noted it has the discretion to direct the enforcement staff to provide an involved individual with full access to the web custodial when "it became apparent during the hearing" the individual "did not have access to all of the pertinent information relating to his allegations maintained in the secure website". *Henderson State University*, Report at pp. 2-3 (July 29, 2014).

According to the committee, a party "has the burden of showing that he was denied reasonable access." *Purdue University, Former Assistant Basketball Coach* at p. 8. For example, if an involved individual contends he or she was denied custodial access to an interview recording of a witness, then a respondent could show the following to satisfy the burden: (a) he or she first received the statement of a witness four days before the response to a notice of allegations was due; (b) the witness's statement or involvement was pertinent to the charges or defenses; (c) the respondent was unable to communicate with the witness in a meaningful way before the response was due; (d) a timely request for a delay in filing the response was made and denied; and (e) as a result, the respondent was unable to present certain pertinent information to the committee on infractions. *Purdue University, Former Assistant Basketball Coach* at p. 8.

Michael L. Buckner

Withdraw of Allegations

The committee on infractions does not commit procedural error by allowing the "enforcement staff to present an allegation that took a considerable time to discuss before the staff ultimately withdrew the allegation" even if "the extended testimony resulted in a reduction of the critical time the institution was afforded to present its case." *University of Texas at El Paso*, Appeals Report No. 140 at p. 9 (January 7, 1998). It is "appropriate for the Committee on Infractions to spend a lengthy period of time reviewing" serious allegations, especially charges involving parties "at risk"; further, "the ultimate decision to withdraw the allegation confirmed that a meaningful dialogue about the issue had occurred." *University of Texas at El Paso* at p. 9. Procedural error did not occur if the record establishes "there was no time limit established for the length of the hearing" and the institution was afforded a "full opportunity to present its position on every facet of the case at the hearing." *University of Texas at El Paso* at p. 9.

Witness Testimony (See Testimony of Witnesses)

EPILOGUE

The NCAA enforcement process can be complex, confusing, and a burden to individuals and institutions. I hope that *The Athletics Investigation Handbook* will assist the reader with conducting internal investigations, responding to NCAA allegations, and preparing for infractions hearings during the enforcement process. By studying the enforcement processes (part 1) and investigative techniques (part 2), learning how to prepare investigative reports (part 3), and reviewing evidentiary and procedural decisions of the committees on infractions (part 4) and the appendices (which feature a glossary, checklists, and a directory of investigative resources), the reader can obtain clarity on important concepts relating to NCAA investigations. Finally, I would be remiss if I did not encourage college administrators, coaches, athletic conference commissioners, attorneys, private investigators, and other professionals facing an allegation to seek the advice of experienced legal counsel when navigating the NCAA enforcement process.

APPENDIX A

INVESTIGATION CHECKLISTS

OUTLINE TO DEVELOP AN ATHLETICS INVESTIGATION POLICY

The following questions are provided to guide an institution through the process of developing an athletics internal investigation policy and procedure:

1. Statement of principle. The policy should build on the institution's core ideology (e.g., core values and purpose). This should cover the institution's goals for promoting NCAA rules compliance and investigating possible violations of NCAA legislation.
    a. What is the institution's definition for all common terms pertaining to internal investigations?
    b. How will the institution express its commitment to rules compliance concerning internal investigations?
    c. What areas of the university community will the policy cover?
    d. To what persons will the policy apply (e.g., administrators, employees, coaches, students, athletic representatives, others)?
2. Legal framework.
    a. What is the relevant NCAA enforcement legislation? Will the institution go further than NCAA legislation in developing its standard operating procedure?
    b. What will be the roles, obligations, and responsibilities of the institution's key actors and stakeholders under the policy?

      c.   How will administrators, employees, coaches, student-athletes, and other persons in the university community be made aware of their policy roles, obligations, and responsibilities?

      d.   What positive action(s) will the institution take in the area of internal investigations?

3.   Policy framework.

      a.   Does the policy provide a framework for other institutional or athletics policies?

      b.   How will other institutional or athletics policies fit with this policy?

      c.   How will the principles in the policy be reflected in related policies and procedures?

4.   Policy development.

      a.   How will the policy be developed and by whom (e.g., planning committee, designated administrator)?

      b.   What training or experience do the members of the committee (or the administrator) have in policy planning?

      c.   How will pertinent constituencies of the university community be involved in the process?

      d.   How will student-athletes be involved in the process?

      e.   What other persons or groups will be consulted about the policy (e.g., legal counsel, campus organizations, experts, stakeholders)?

      f.   How will the institution ensure full commitment to the policy and to its implementation?

      g.   How will the institution review and audit the policy? What outside entity will evaluate the policy at least once every four years?

      h.   What procedures and forms should be revised or created during this process?

      i.   What will be the institution's statement or policy regarding specific internal investigation areas?

      j.   A statement of the institution's internal investigation philosophy.

      k.   A description of the method used to develop the policies.

    l. A description of the educational component.

    m. A statement of the responsibilities of involved institutional personnel.

    n. Internal investigation-related forms.

    o. Communication of an internal investigation and its findings to the NCAA enforcement staff and the conference office.

5. Monitoring and education.

    a. How will the institution ensure that each area of the policy is incorporated into the rules education, staff orientation, and professional development programs?

    b. What steps will be taken to ensure that all persons have access to education, training, and support so that they can fulfill their responsibilities under the policy?

    c. How will the policy be communicated to the university community (e.g., newsletter, compliance presentations at organizational meetings, conference call, and web-based seminars, websites, intranet, e-mail)?

    d. How will the institution monitor and evaluate the effectiveness of its rules education, staff orientation, and professional development programs concerning the policy?

6. Policy implementation and follow-up.

    a. How will the institution's legal counsel or other appropriate campus offices provide appropriate input?

    b. How will the chief executive officer provide input before approving the policy?

    c. How will the policy be put into practice?

    d. What action plans and targets will be created for policy implementation, and when will the plans and targets be reviewed (e.g., annually, semi-annually)?

    e. Who will be responsible for the action plan and target implementation?

    f. Where will the policy be filed for official purposes?

PRELIMINARY DETERMINATION CHECKLIST

A preliminary determination is a discussion or a series of discussions concerning investigation planning involving the institution and the internal investigator at the start of an internal investigation. Issues that should be addressed during the preliminary determination include:

- Legal and factual issues expected to be encountered during the investigation.
- Potential legal exposure and NCAA sanctions faced by the institution.
- Location, number, and identity of the key documents to be reviewed.
- Identities and locations of key persons to be interviewed.
- Coordination of the communication of the institution's investigation to the NCAA enforcement staff and to athletic conference officials.
- Organization of the reporting and supervising scheme for the investigation.
- Contingency measures.
- Identities of additional persons, experts, or groups to assist the investigator.
- Agreement on the scope and goals of the investigation.

INVESTIGATION PLAN CHECKLIST

Contents of an Investigation Plan

- Documentation of the conclusions reached during the preliminary determination.
- Issues, topics, and matters to be examined during the investigation.
- Detailed investigative task list, including:
    - Identification of responsibilities for each investigation team member.
    - Estimate of time line (i.e., anticipated start and completion dates) for each investigative task.
- Plan and procedure for client-investigator communication.
- Identification of staff, areas, offices, and departments that will be involved in the investigation.
- Identification of expertise of logistical support required by the investigator.
- Expected fees and costs.
- Milestones and report dates.
- Possible outcomes.

Reminders

- Submit the plan for review and approval by the institution's chief executive officer or the person at the institution to whom the internal investigator reports.
- Review the plan periodically during the inquiry.
- Revise the plan when additional information or feedback is obtained during the investigation.

FIVE-STEP EVIDENCE COLLECTION PLAN

1. Retain.
    - Review (and possibly suspend aspects of) the institution's document destruction policy and e-mail deletion program.
2. Appoint.
    - Appoint a document custodian and/or an electronic document custodian, if needed.
3. Conduct.
    - Conduct evidence searches in pertinent campus locations.
    - Send written requests for evidence to institutional personnel, student-athletes, and athletic representatives.
4. Collect.
    - Collect and record evidence.
5. Identify.
    - Identify, collect, and record additional evidence developed through further questioning of persons and/or analysis of existing evidence.

EVIDENCE IDENTIFICATION CHECKLIST

All evidence should be marked with a Bates stamp, a document number, or some other form of identification. Information should include:

- Time and date that the document was processed as evidence.
- Name of the investigator.
- Name of the person who produced or possessed the evidence.
- Location where the evidence was found.

Reminders

- Identification marks for sensitive evidence should be placed on the evidence bag and not directly on the evidence.
- Contact a local law enforcement agency to collect evidence relevant to the commission of a crime.

PRIVILEGE-LOG CHECKLIST

A privilege log describes the documents not produced by an institution to the NCAA enforcement staff because of a legal privilege. A typical privilege log contains the following information for each document:

- Bates stamp or document number assigned to the document.
- Date of the document.
- Type of document (e.g., letter, memorandum, report).
- Author of the document.
- Recipient of the document, including persons who received carbon copies (cc) and blind carbon copies (bcc).
- Type of privilege claimed (e.g., attorney-client, attorney work-product, self-evaluative).

PRE-INTERVIEW TASK CHECKLIST

The following checklist details the items that should be completed by the investigator prior to an interview of a subject.

1. Confirm the date, time, and location of the scheduled interview with all involved individuals, including, but not limited to, the NCAA enforcement staff (if conducting a joint investigation).
2. Review the investigation plan.
3. Review the investigation chart.
4. Review memoranda, reports, and notes of prior interviews.
5. Review relevant documents and other evidence.
6. Prepare an outline of the interview questions.
7. Prepare a contingency plan to address issues that may arise during the interview.
8. Makes copies of any documents that will be used during the interview.
9. Coordinate pertinent activities with involved individuals (e.g., court reporter, interview room reservation).

INTERVIEW MATERIALS CHECKLIST

The following checklist details the materials that should be brought by the investigator to the interview.

1. Notepads and writing instruments.
2. Recording device and extra batteries.
3. Labels (to note the date and time of evidence produced during the interview).
4. Copy of NCAA legislation, institutional rules, and federal and state laws.
5. Interview outline.
6. Copies of relevant documents for the interview subject and other persons sitting in on the interview.
7. Blank copies of the interview notice/statement of confidentiality and other forms.
8. Documentation to identify the investigator to the interview subject.
9. Any other item needed to conduct the interview.

SAMPLE INTERVIEW NOTICE

You are advised of the following:

- The purpose of the interview is to determine whether you have knowledge of, or have been involved, directly or indirectly, in any violation of NCAA, conference, and/or university rules and regulations.
- You have an affirmative obligation to cooperate fully with and assist the NCAA, conference and/or university—which includes protecting the integrity of the investigation—and to make a full and complete disclosure of any relevant information, including any information requested by the university, the conference, the enforcement staff, or the infractions committees.
- You have an affirmative obligation to report instances of noncompliance to the NCAA, conference, and/or university in a timely manner and to assist in developing full information to determine whether a possible violation has occurred and the details thereof.
- Exemplary cooperation by you may constitute a mitigating factor for purposes of calculating a penalty when a violation has occurred.
- Failing to satisfy the responsibility to cooperate may result in an independent allegation and/or be considered an aggravating factor for purposes of calculating a penalty.
- Refusing to furnish information or providing false or misleading information to the NCAA, conference, and/or the university may result in an allegation that you have violated NCAA, conference, and/or university ethical-conduct rules.

- The interview is confidential pursuant to NCAA, conference, and/or university rules and regulations. In other words, with the exception of your legal counsel, you may not disclose the substance of this interview to any third party, including other employees or anyone outside of the university.
- You have the right to have legal counsel present during the interview.

I hereby acknowledge:

- I reviewed and understood the purpose of the interview as well as my rights and obligations under NCAA, conference, and/or university rules and regulations.
- Any statement I make can be used in any NCAA, NCAA Eligibility Center, conference, and/or university proceeding.
- If it is found that I was involved directly or indirectly in any violation of NCAA, conference, and/or university rules and regulations, any statement I make can affect adversely my eligibility at, or employment or affiliation with, the university.
- I can be subject to disciplinary or corrective action under NCAA, conference, and/or university rules and regulations should I fail to abide by the above-stated principles.

_____	_____
Interview Subject Name (Print)	Witness Name (Print)
_____	_____
Interview Subject's Signature	Witness's Signature
_____	_____
Date and Time of Subject's Signature	Date and Time of Witness's Signature

DOCUMENT REQUEST/ PRODUCTION CHECKLIST

An investigator should request evidence relevant to an allegation. The following checklist contains a nonexhaustive list of information that may be relevant during an internal investigation of an alleged NCAA rules violation.

1. Athletics-related policies of the university governing board (e.g., board of trustees).
2. Employee handbooks and manuals.
3. Athletics operational manual.
4. Athletics compliance manual.
5. Student-athlete handbook.
6. Telephone and cell phone records.
7. E-mail messages.
8. Text messages.
9. Postings to university bulletin boards (e.g., electronic, office corkboard).
10. Correspondence (e.g., letters, memos, notecards).
11. The personnel file of the target and other pertinent employees.
12. Student file for the involved student-athletes:
    a. Academic file.
    b. Athletics compliance file.
    c. Athletics training records.
13. Reports, complaints, or allegations filed by the accuser.
14. Coach's practice plans and scripts.
15. Video and film records of athletics-related activities.

16. Sports team's policies, procedures, and rules (e.g., team rules).
17. Documentation of education and training provided to student-athletes and coaches.
18. E-mails and other electronic information submitted.
19. Compliance forms (e.g., countable athletics-related activities logs, recruiting logs).
20. Rules education records (e.g., agendas, handouts, PowerPoint presentation slides, attendance records).
21. Self-reports of NCAA rules violations.
22. Athletics compliance audit reports.
23. Head coach monitoring documentation (for allegations involving a head coach or members of a team).
24. Allegations, complaints, or comments reported to the university related to the allegation.
25. Commendations of the target and other pertinent employees.
26. Documents signed by the employees involved (such as hiring agreements, employment contracts, and other agreements).
27. Expense reports.
28. Computer records (e.g., Internet sites visited, productivity).
29. Files from any previous investigations of the same employees or the same type of allegations.

INTERNAL INVESTIGATION REPORT CHECKLIST

An institution prepares a written self-report after a comprehensive and objective internal investigation into alleged NCAA rules violations. A self-report resulting from an investigation of a Level I and II (Division I) or a major (Divisions II and III) case should include, at a minimum, nine main sections:

1. Introduction.
    a. Purpose of the report.
    b. Case chronology.
2. Overview of the findings.
    a. Identification of the types of rules violations and persons involved.
    b. List and brief bios of all involved individuals and parties.
    c. List of, and eligibility information for, involved student-athletes.
3. Summary of the institution's internal investigation.
    a. Investigation methodology.
    b. List of interview subjects.
    c. Summary of evidence collected.
4. Findings of specific rules violations.
    a. NCAA legislation involved in the violation.
    b. Date of the violation.
    c. Location of the violation.
    d. Description of the violation.
    e. Who was involved in the violation.

        f.   How the violation was discovered.

        g.   Summary of the information developed during the institution's internal investigation.

        h.   Mitigating and aggravating factors.

        i.   Cause of the violation.

5.   Possible rules violations.

        a.   List of possible rules violations that were investigated but the evidence revealed did not occur.

        b.   List of possible rules violations that were investigated but for which the evidence was inconclusive.

6.   Self-corrective measures and self-imposed penalties.

        a.   Measures undertaken to correct or to strengthen the athletics program.

        b.   Penalties implemented by the school or conference.

7.   Background information on the institution and athletics program.

        a.   History of the university.

        b.   NCAA division.

        c.   Conference membership(s).

        d.   Number of NCAA-sponsored sports.

        e.   Overview of the institution's history of Level I, Level II, and major infractions.

8.   Conclusion.

        a.   Summation of the institution's internal investigation.

        b.   Comments on the institution's commitment to rules compliance, institutional control, or other NCAA-imposed duty.

        c.   Miscellaneous information.

9.   Appendix.

        a.   Athletics-related information needed to process the report (e.g., squad lists, practice logs).

        b.   Important documents obtained during the investigation.

TIPS TO AVOID INTERNAL INVESTIGATION ERRORS

An institution prepares a written self-report after a comprehensive and objective internal investigation into alleged NCAA rules violations. The following are tips to avoid the most common errors in conducting an internal investigation and preparing the self-report:

1. Follow the institution's written internal investigation policy and procedure.
2. Maintain accurate records of all investigation interviews and evidence collected.
3. Recognize and address all student-athlete eligibility issues during the internal investigation and in the self-report.
4. Provide all student-athletes, institutional employees, and athletics representatives (boosters) a notice of their NCAA Bylaw 10.1 (ethical conduct) obligations prior to an investigation interview.
5. Submit all relevant information, including pertinent documents, data, and evidence that corroborate or refute the alleged rules violation, in the self-report.
6. In the self-report, state the specific NCAA Bylaw that was violated.
7. Develop evidence to demonstrate the existence of mitigating factors and to address the occurrence of aggravating factors.
8. In the self-report, identify who reported the allegation.
9. In the self-report, describe the institution's self-corrective measures and self-imposed penalties relating to the reported violations.
10. Document (through a report or memorandum) if the internal investigation determines no rules violation occurred.

APPENDIX B
GLOSSARY

aggravating factors. Circumstances that warrant a higher range of penalties in a case, including, but not limited to, multiple Level I violations by the institution or involved individual; a history of Level I, Level II, or major violations by the institution, sport program(s), or involved individual; lack of institutional control; obstructing an investigation or attempting to conceal unethical conduct; compromising the integrity of an investigation; failing to cooperate during an investigation or refusing to provide all relevant or requested information; violations were premeditated, deliberate, or committed after substantial planning; multiple Level II violations by the institution or involved individual; persons of authority condoned, participated in, or negligently disregarded the violation or related wrongful conduct; one or more violations caused significant ineligibility or other substantial harm to a student-athlete or a prospective student-athlete; conduct or circumstances demonstrating an abuse of a position of trust; a pattern of noncompliance within the sport program(s) involved; conduct intended to generate pecuniary gain for the institution or involved individual; intentional, willful, or blatant disregard for the NCAA Constitution and bylaws; other facts warranting a higher penalty range.

appeals committee. See *infractions appeals committee.*

association. See *National Collegiate Athletic Association.*

athletic conference. A group of colleges and/or universities that conducts competition among its member and determines a conference champion in one or more sports.

athletic representative. See *representative of the institution's athletics interests.*

attorney-client privilege. A legal doctrine that allows a client to refuse to disclose and to prevent any other person from disclosing confidential communications between the client and the client's attorney.

breach of conduct. One or more violations that are isolated or limited in nature, provide no more than a minimal recruiting, competitive, or other advantage, and provide no more than a minimal impermissible benefit.

bylaw. A rule that governs the operations of the NCAA and its members. Bylaws are introduced and voted on by division-specific boards, councils, and committees made up of representatives from the NCAA membership. Some bylaws are common among all divisions, while others are applicable only to members in a specific division. Bylaws are published annually in a division-specific NCAA manual. Bylaws can also be accessed on the NCAA website (http://www.ncaa.org).

chain of custody. The process applied to the handling of evidence in an investigation. Because evidence collected during an investigation can be used by an institution and involved individuals in an infractions hearing to support or deny allegations, it must be handled in a deliberate manner to avoid claims of inauthenticity, tampering, or misconduct. The chain of custody is established when the investigator collects a piece of evidence, documents its collection, and stores it in a secure place. Chain of custody is maintained when every activity between the collection of evidence and its appearance at an infractions hearing is completely documented.

chief executive officer. A person (generally, a president or chancellor) responsible for implementation of the strategic plan and policies established by the institutional or university system board of trustees/regents. The chief executive officer also oversees the institution's operations. Under NCAA legislation, a chief executive officer has the ultimate responsibility and authority for the conduct of an institution's athletic program.

committees on infractions. Independent bodies composed of individuals from NCAA member institutions, athletic conferences, and the general public. Each NCAA division has its own committee on infractions. The committees are responsible for administration of the NCAA enforcement program. The committees have the authority to: (a) consider compliance concerning a member's failure to maintain NCAA academic or athletic standards or membership conditions or obligations; (b) devise and amend policies and procedures for the NCAA enforcement process; (c) establish facts related to alleged violations and discover violations of NCAA legislation; (d) impose an appropriate penalty or show-cause requirement on a member found to be involved in a major violation (or in appeals involving secondary violations) or recommend suspension or termination of membership to the division-specific board of directors or president's council; and (e) carry out any other duties directly related to the administration of the enforcement process.

committee on infractions hearing. See *hearing.*

competition penalties. Competition limitations on the institution's participation in postseason play in the involved sport(s).

compliance officer. A person employed to coordinate the administration of an institution's athletic compliance program.

conference. See *athletic conference.*

conference commissioner. A person charged with overseeing the operations of an athletic conference.

coordinator of appeals. A member of a committee on infractions who represents the committee on matters appealed to an infractions appeals committee.

custodial site. A location (established within the period specified by NCAA legislation or internal procedures) where a member institution or involved individual is provided reasonable access to the NCAA enforcement staff's copies of tape-recorded interviews, interview summaries, interview transcripts, and other evidentiary information pertinent to an infractions case. The enforcement staff provides the institution and involved individuals with access to the information through a secure website or at the NCAA national office.

director of athletics. A person responsible for the operations of an institution's athletics program.

director of enforcement. An NCAA staff member who assists the vice president for enforcement services. A director of enforcement supervises a team of associate and assistant directors, as well as other staff, that investigates alleged violations of NCAA legislation.

document custodian. An institutional employee who assists an internal investigator with the collection of evidence. The document custodian's duties include: (a) directing employees, students, and athletic representatives to search for and deliver (or inform the custodian of the location of) requested documents and files; and (b) serving as a contact point inside the institution to coordinate these efforts.

electronic document custodian. An institutional employee who assists an internal investigator with the collection of electronic evidence. The electronic document custodian's duties consist of searching handheld devises, smartphones, computers, computer disks and storage units, and other electronic files owned and operated by the institution.

enforcement process. See *NCAA enforcement process.*

enforcement program. See *NCAA enforcement process.*

enforcement staff case summary. A document prepared by the NCAA enforcement staff prior to a committee on infractions hearing. The case summary lists the allegations, the position of the institution and involved individuals on each allegation, any remaining issues, the identities of individuals involved in the case, and any other pertinent information. The case summary is provided to the institution, involved individuals, and the committee on infractions no later than two weeks before the hearing.

evidence log. A document or system that lists the evidence collected during an internal investigation.

faculty athletics representative. A member of an institution's faculty or administrative staff who is designated by the chief executive officer to represent the institution and its faculty in the institution's relationships with the NCAA and its athletic conference.

financial penalties. Financial penalties may include requirements that an institution pay a fine, return revenue received from a specific athletic event or series of events, or face a reduction in or elimination of monetary distribution by the NCAA.

head coach restrictions. If a determination is made by the committee on infractions that an employing institution has not taken appropriate disciplinary or corrective action regarding a head coach found in violation of Bylaw 11.1.2.1, the committee may issue an order that the institution suspend the coach for a number of contests from the range set forth in legislation that would apply to the underlying violation(s) unless the institution appears before the panel to show cause why the suspension should not be applied. Decisions regarding disciplinary or corrective actions involving personnel are made by the institution, but the determination of whether the action satisfies the institution's obligation of NCAA membership rests solely with the committee on infractions.

hearing. A proceeding before a committee on infractions or an infractions appeals committee in which evidence and argument are presented by the NCAA enforcement staff, a member institution, involved individuals, and (in a hearing before an appeals committee) the committee on infractions to determine specific findings concerning allegations of NCAA rules violations and penalties, if any.

hearing panel. In Division I, all cases involving Level I or II violations will be presented to, and decided by, hearing panels of no less than five and no more than seven members of the committee on infractions. The decisions reached by hearing panels are made on behalf of the committee.

incidental infraction. In Division I, a minor infraction that is technical in nature and does not constitute a Level III violation. Incidental infractions generally will not affect eligibility for intercollegiate athletics. Multiple or repeated Level IV violations collectively may constitute a Level III violation.

infraction. A violation of an NCAA or athletic conference bylaw or rule.

infraction appeals committees. Independent bodies composed of individuals from NCAA member institutions, athletic conferences, and the general public. Each NCAA division has its own appeals committee. The committees are charged with hearing and deciding on appeals concerning the findings of major violations by each division's committee on infractions.

infractions appeals report. See *infractions reports.*

infractions case. The proceedings and activities, including the investigation and infractions hearing, to determine whether a member institution is in noncompliance with NCAA legislation.

infractions hearing. See *hearing.*

infractions report. A document that outlines the specific findings made and penalties imposed by a committee on infractions or infractions appeals committee as well as the rationale for the committee's decision.

inquiry. See *investigation.*

internal investigation. A detailed inquiry or systematic examination of an alleged violation(s) of federal or state law, NCAA legislation, athletic conference rules, or institutional regulations that is conducted by a member institution into its athletic program.

internal investigator. The person or committee conducting an internal investigation on behalf of an institution.

investigation. A detailed inquiry or systematic examination of an alleged violation(s) of federal or state law, NCAA legislation, athletic conference rules, or institutional regulations.

investigation chart. A document that contains the associations of people and organizations, as well as important events, involved in the alleged violation.

investigation management file. A system used by an internal investigator to document, file, and maintain information collected during an investigation. The file consists of: (a) a means to catalog the information, using a computer system, filing system, or card reference system; and (b) a secure place to store the information.

investigation plan. A document that maps out the strategy and steps involved in an inquiry.

involved individual. Current or former institutional staff members and current or former student-athletes who have received notice of involvement in alleged violations.

involved party. See *involved individual.*

legislation. See *bylaw.*

Level I violation. See *severe breach of conduct.*

Level II violation. See *significant breach of conduct.*

Level III violation. See *breach of conduct.*

Level IV violation. See *incidental infraction.*

major violation. A violation of NCAA legislation that is not deemed a secondary violation and includes any infraction that provides an extensive recruiting or competitive advantage.

member institution. See *NCAA member institution.*

mitigating factors. Circumstances that warrant a lower range of penalties in a case. A hearing panel of the committee on infractions determines whether mitigating factors are present in a case and the weight assigned to each factor. Examples of mitigating factors include but are not limited to the following: prompt self-detection and self-disclosure of the violation(s); prompt acknowledgment of the violation, acceptance of responsibility and (for an institution) imposition of meaningful corrective measures and/ or penalties; affirmative steps to expedite final resolution of the matter; an established history of self-reporting Level III or secondary violations; implementation of a system of compliance methods designed to ensure rules compliance and satisfaction of institutional/coach control standards; exemplary cooperation; the violations were unintentional, limited in scope, and represent a deviation from otherwise compliant practices by the institution or involved individual; other facts warranting a lower penalty range.

National Collegiate Athletic Association. A voluntary association of about 1,200 colleges and universities, athletic conferences, and sports organizations devoted to the sound administration of intercollegiate athletics.

NCAA. See *National Collegiate Athletic Association.*

NCAA enforcement process. A program that addresses instances of noncompliance with NCAA legislation by an NCAA member institution. The enforcement process is designed to be a cooperative program involving member institutions, involved individuals, athletic conferences, and the NCAA enforcement staff to: (a) reduce secondary and major violations of NCAA legislation; and (b) impose appropriate corrective measures and penalties if violations occur at an institution.

NCAA enforcement program. See *NCAA enforcement process.*

NCAA member institution. A college or university that has a membership in the NCAA. A member institution is classified in either Divisions I, II, or III.

new evidence. Relevant material information that could not reasonably have been ascertained prior to a committee on infractions hearing.

notice of allegations. A document issued by the NCAA enforcement staff to a member institution's president or chancellor after the staff determines that sufficient information exists to believe that a major violation occurred at the institution. A notice of allegations contains specific allegations of NCAA rules violations against an institution.

notice of inquiry. A document issued by the NCAA enforcement staff to a member institution's president or chancellor that informs the institution of the staff's investigation of alleged violations of NCAA legislation. A notice of inquiry also may indicate: (a) the involved sports; (b) the nature of the potential violations; (c) the approximate time period in which the alleged violations occurred; (d) the identities of the involved individuals; (e) the approximate time frame for the investigation; and (f) a statement that other facts may be developed during the investigation that may relate to additional violations.

preliminary determination. A series of discussions concerning investigation planning involving the institution and the internal investigator at the start of an internal investigation. A preliminary determination should address: (a) legal and factual issues expected to be encountered during the investigation; (b) potential legal exposure and NCAA sanctions faced by the institution; (c) location, volume, and identity of the key documents to be reviewed; (d) identities and locations of key persons to be interviewed; (e) coordination of the communication of the institution's investigation to the NCAA enforcement staff and athletic conference officials; (f) organization of the reporting and supervising scheme for the investigation; (g) contingency measures; (h) identities of additional persons, experts, or groups to assist the internal investigator; and (i) scope and goals of the investigation.

privilege log. A document submitted by an institution that lists the documents not produced to the NCAA enforcement staff because of a legal privilege.

probation. The hearing panel may prescribe probationary conditions designed on a case-by-case basis to remedy weaknesses detected in the institution's administration of its athletics programs. Prior to expiration of the probation period and before the institution is restored to full rights and privileges of NCAA membership, the office of the committees on infractions will review the athletics policies and practices of the institution. If an institution fails to satisfy all probationary conditions, the committee may extend the probationary period and/or prescribe additional penalties.

recruiting restrictions. Recruiting restrictions may include limitations for varying lengths of time on official visits, unofficial visits (the number of scheduled unofficial visits, provision of complimentary admissions and local transportation), recruiting communications (telephone and written correspondence), and off-campus recruiting activities.

representation of the institution's athletics interests. An individual, independent agency, corporate entity, or other organization that is known, or that should have been known, by a member of the institution's administration to: (a) have participated in or been a member of an agency or organization promoting the institution's athletic program; (b) have made financial contributions to the athletic department or to an athletic booster organization of the institution; (c) be assisting or to have been requested by athletic staff to assist in the recruitment of prospective student-athletes; (d) be assisting or have assisted in providing benefits to enrolled student-athletes or their families; or (e) have been involved otherwise in promoting the institution's athletic program. An individual, independent agency, corporate entity, or other organization identified as an athletic representative retains that identity indefinitely.

secondary violation. A violation of NCAA legislation that is isolated or inadvertent in nature, provides or is intended to provide only a minimal recruiting, competitive, or other advantage, and does not include any significant recruiting inducement or extra benefit. The NCAA can consider the occurrence of multiple secondary violations a major violation.

scholarship reductions. Limitations on the number of financial aid awards that may be provided during a specified period.

self-disclosure. A type of self-report submitted to the NCAA enforcement staff when the institution uncovers a violation before it was reported to the institution's athletic conference or to the enforcement staff.

self-evaluative privilege. A legal doctrine that has been applied by some federal courts and states to protect an organization's internal review of its operations. A federal court has determined that the privilege applies to documents that satisfy a five-part test: (a) the information for which the privilege is sought must result from critical self-analysis by the party seeking to invoke the privilege; (b) the public must have a strong interest in preserving the free flow of the information at issue; (c) the flow of the information would be curtailed if discovery were allowed; (d) the information must have been prepared with the expectation that it would remain confidential; and (e) the information concerns only a subjective analysis and not statistical or objective factual material. *Reid v. Lockheed Martin Aeronautics Co.,* 199 F.R.D. 379, 386 (N.D. Ga. 2001).

self-report. The document provided by an institution to the NCAA enforcement staff that reports secondary or major violations of NCAA legislation that have already been reported to the institution's athletic conference or to the NCAA enforcement staff.

senior woman administrator. The highest-ranking female administrator involved with the conduct of a member institution's athletic program.

sensitive evidence. Evidence that will be submitted to an outside expert or laboratory for forensic analysis.

severe breach of conduct. One or more violations that seriously undermine or threaten the integrity of the NCAA collegiate model as set forth in the constitution and bylaws, including any violation that provides or is intended to provide a substantial or extensive recruiting, competitive, or other advantage, or a substantial or extensive impermissible benefit.

show-cause orders. If a determination is made by the committee on infractions that an employing institution has not taken appropriate disciplinary or corrective action regarding a head coach found in violation of Bylaw 11.1.2.1, the committee may issue an order that the institution suspend the coach for a number of contests from the range set forth in legislation that would apply to the underlying violation(s) unless the institution appears before the panel to show cause why the suspension should not be applied. Decisions regarding disciplinary or corrective actions involving personnel are made by the institution, but the determination of whether the action satisfies the institution's obligation of NCAA membership rests solely with the committee on infractions.

significant breach of conduct. One or more violations that provide or are intended to provide more than a minimal but less than a substantial or extensive recruiting, competitive, or other advantage; these include more than a minimal but less than a substantial or extensive impermissible benefit or involve conduct that may compromise the integrity of the NCAA collegiate model as set forth in the constitution and bylaws.

special investigative committee. A body composed of administrators, faculty members, staff, and other persons with relevant expertise that is created by a member institution to investigate alleged violations of NCAA legislation and institutional rules in an athletic program. A special investigative committee also refers to a body composed of noninstitutional personnel and experts who are appointed by an institution's chief executive officer or an elected official to investigate alleged violations of federal and state law, institutional rules, and/or NCAA legislation in the athletic program.

student-athlete. A student who: (a) was recruited by an institution or an athletic representative to participate in the institution's athletic program; or (b) reports for an intercollegiate athletic team that is under the jurisdiction of the institution's athletic program.

summary disposition. A procedure used in place of a formal committee hearing. The summary disposition procedure requires the NCAA enforcement staff, the member institution, and involved individuals to agree with the facts of a case and stipulate that the facts constitute major violations of NCAA legislation. The member institution and involved individuals also propose penalties that address the stipulated violations. The committee on infractions has the authority to: (a) approve the agreed-upon findings and proposed penalties; (b) not approve the findings (which will result in a hearing); (c) not approve the proposed penalties (which can result in an expedited hearing); or (d) request additional information.

vice president for enforcement services. A person responsible for the operations of the NCAA enforcement services group.

work-product doctrine. A legal doctrine that protects notes, working documents, memoranda, or other materials prepared by an attorney in anticipation of litigation.

BIBLIOGRAPHY

American Association of Fundraising Counsel. "How to Choose Counsel." Glenview, Illinois: AAFC, 2004. http://www.aafrc.org/choose_counsel/ (accessed July 9, 2004).

Boese, John T. "Internal Investigations After Sarbanes-Oxley: Best Practices in Avoiding Obstruction of Justice." Washington, D.C.: Fried, Frank, Harris, Shriver & Jacobson LLP, 2002. http://www.ffhsj.com/symposium_material/gc_fall_02/internal_investigations_sox.pdf (accessed July 9, 2004).

Buckner, Michael L. "Conducting Internal Investigations: Legal, Ethical and Compliance Issues in NCAA Enforcement Cases." Presentation during Holland & Knight Institute videoconference, Jacksonville, Florida, June 21, 2002.

Clark, Franklin and Diliberto, Ken. *Investigating Computer Crime.* New York: CRC Press, 1996.

Clark, Lana J. "Privilege Issues During Discovery." *RECAP* (Spring 1999). http://www.caparalegal.org/PDF%20Files/207348.pdf (accessed July 9, 2004).

Columbia Law Review, and others, eds. *The Bluebook: A Uniform System of Citation.* 17th ed. Cambridge, Massachusetts: Harvard Law Review Association, 2000.

Committees on Infractions, National Collegiate Athletic Association. *Procedures Followed During Hearings Before the Committee on Infractions.* Indianapolis, Indiana: NCAA, 2003.

Division I Committee on Infractions, National Collegiate Athletic Association. *Principles of Institutional Control.* Indianapolis, Indiana: NCAA, 1996. http://www.ncaa.org/databases/regional_seminars/

guide_rules_compliance/other_topics/oth_01.html (accessed July 12, 2004).

Division I Infractions Appeals Committee, National Collegiate Athletic Association. *NCAA Division I Infractions Appeals Committee Policies and Procedures Guide*. Indianapolis, Indiana: NCAA, 2003. http://www1. ncaa.org/membership/governance/division_I/infractions_appeals/ index.html (accessed July 9, 2004).

Davis, Seth. "Biggest lessons learned at NCAA's Enforcement Experience." SI.com (May 12, 2011). http://www.si.com/more-sports/2011/05/12/ ncaa-enforcement (accessed July 13, 2014).

Dodd, Dennis. "'Transparent' NCAA shows how enforcement sausage is made." CBSSports.com (May 13, 2011). http://www.cbssports. com/collegefootball/story/15060997/transparent-ncaa-shows-how- enforcement-sausage-is-made (accessed July 13, 2014).

Enforcement/Infractions, National Collegiate Athletic Association. "Frequently Asked Questions about the NCAA Enforcement Process." Indianapolis, Indiana: NCAA, 2004. http://www.ncaa.org/ enforcefrontF.html (accessed July 9, 2004).

Enforcement Services Group, National Collegiate Athletic Association. *Guidelines for NCAA Member Institutions Submitting Results of Internal Inquiries Concerning Possible Major Violations*. Indianapolis, Indiana: NCAA, 2001.

Evans, Mary Margaret and Pamela A. Stagner. "Maintaining the Chain of Custody: Evidence Handling in Forensic Cases." *AORN Journal* 78 (October 2003).

Florida Bar, The. "How to Find a Lawyer in Florida." Tallahassee, Florida: Florida Bar 2003. http://www.flabar.org/TFB/TFBConsum.nsf/0/ e68cff728f0c46d485256b2f006c5cb4?OpenDocument (accessed July 9, 2004).

Forensic Telecourse Development Committee, California Commission on Peace Officer Standards and Training. "Crime Scene Response Guidelines." Workbook presented for the Forensic Technology for Law Enforcement Telecourse, n.l., May 13, 1993. Adapted in *Evidence Collection Guidelines*. Temecula, California: www.crime-scene- investigator.net, n.d. http://www.crime-scene-investigator.net/collect. html#11 (accessed July 11, 2004).

Guerin, Lisa. *Workplace Investigations: A Step-by-Step Guide.* Berkeley, California: Nolo, 2004.

Kinnee, Kevin B. *Practical Investigation Techniques.* Boca Raton, Florida: CRC Press, 1994.

Kuehne, Benedict P. "Protecting the Privilege in the Corporate Setting: Conducting and Defending Internal Corporate Internal Investigations." *St. Thomas Law Review* 9, no. 651 (1997).

Lynch, Gary G. and Douglas M. Fuchs. "Conducting Internal Investigations of Possible Corporate Wrongdoing." *PLI Corporate Law and Practice Course Handbook Series* 943 (1996).

Marsh, Gene and Marie Robbins. "Weighing the Interests of the Institution, the Membership and Institutional Representatives in an NCAA Investigation." *Florida Law Review* 55, no. 667 (2003).

Marshall, Raymond C. "Conducting Internal Investigations: What to Do and Not Do." *ALI-ABA Course of Study* (1999).

Morrison, Edgar C. "What Happens When You Are the Target of an Investigation?" San Antonio, Texas: Jackson Walker L.L.P., 1999. http://www.jw.com/site/jsp/publicationinfo.jsp?id=146 (accessed July 9, 2004).

National Collegiate Athletic Association. *2013-14 NCAA Divisions I, II, and III Manuals.* Indianapolis, Indiana: NCAA, 2013.

National Collegiate Athletic Association. *2014-15 NCAA Divisions I, II, and III Manuals.* Indianapolis, Indiana: NCAA, 2014.

National Collegiate Athletic Association. "What is the NCAA?" Indianapolis, Indiana: NCAA, n.d. http://www.ncaa.org/ (accessed July 10, 2004).

Nicholson, Larry G. *Security Investigations: A Professional's Guide.* Boston: Butterworth-Heinemann, 2000.

Patzakis, John. "Maintaining the Digital Chain of Custody." Dayton, Ohio: Infosecurity Europe, 2003. http://www.infosec.co.uk/files/guidance_software_04_12_03.pdf (accessed July 9, 2004).

Poteet, Dewey. *How to Conduct an Effective Workplace Investigation.* Austin, Texas: Akin, Gump, Strauss, Hauer & Feld LLP, 2001. http://www.akingump.com/docs/publication/ 293.pdf (accessed July 9, 2004).

Potuto, Josephine R., "A Panel Discussion: Self-Discovery and Investigations." Paper presented at the 2004 NCAA Regional Rules

Compliance Seminars, Anaheim, California, Indianapolis, Indiana, and New York City, New York, May 6, May 20, and June 3, 2004.

Solomon, Jon. "Mock NCAA inquiry sheds light on confusing enforcement process." al.com (May 13, 2011). http://www.al.com/sports/index. ssf/2011/05/mock_ncaa_inquiry_sheds_light.html (last visited July 13, 2014).